The Freshwater Fish Cookbook

The Freshwater Fish Cookbook

More than 200 Ways to Cook Your Catch

A.D. LIVINGSTON

THE LYONS PRESS
Guilford, Connecticut

An imprint of The Globe Pequot Press

The Lyons Press is an imprint of The Globe Pequot Press

Designed by Sheryl P. Kober

Photos on pp. ix, 38, 61, 97, 100, 121, 152, and 173 © Shutterstock. All others by Monte Burch

Library of Congress Cataloging-in-Publication Data
Livingston, A. D., 1932-
the freshwater fish cookbook : more than 200 ways to cook your catch / A.D. Livingston.
p. cm.
Includes bibliographical references and index.
ISBN 978-1-59921-386-6 (alk. paper)
1. Cookery (Fish) 2. Freshwater fishes. I. Title. II. Title: Freshwater fish cookbook.
TX747.L568 2009
641.6'92—dc22

2008020204

Printed in China

10 9 8 7 6 5 4 3 2 1

For Jeff, Bill, James, and Jarrod

Other Books by A.D. Livingston

Venison Cookbook

Jerky

Cold-Smoking and Salt-Curing Meat, Fish, & Game

Sausage

The Complete Fish & Game Cookbook

Cast-Iron Cooking

The Whole Grains Cookbook

Skillet Cooking for Camp and Kitchen

Contents

Introduction

I applaud those anglers who practice the catch-and-release policy, but I must ask them to remember that putting food on the table is, atavistically, what fishing is all about. In most cases, keeping a few to eat won't hurt the fishery. Those amongst us who feel guilty about keeping a trout or two should perhaps also target, by way of bonus angling, bluegills, crappie, whitefish, and other species that are quite plentiful, fun to catch, and tasty. Some of these species are stunted by overpopulation and should be thinned out. So, catch enough to feed family and friends. Be warned, however, that a 10-pound tackle-busting grinnel or a 3-foot snakehead might well change a few minds about what is and is not a "game fish."

Most young anglers are especially proud of eating their catch, and they often become more avid fishermen and better conservationists because of the experience. Don't disappoint them.

Also let me say that the angler has the best of fish cookery. In spite of aquaculturists' propaganda and a few misinformed writers to the contrary, river fish don't taste muddy. In short, the angler worth his salt can catch a better fish than he can buy. At least he will know what kind of fish he has, what sort of water it came from, and, importantly, how fresh it is. The skilled angler can also get enough to eat—which is hard to do in many swanky restaurants these days.

Hopefully, this book will help the angler find a suitable recipe or two for the catch. That's why the chapters are organized by specific fish instead of on frying, baking, and other cooking techniques. Most of the recipes are easy to prepare and don't require a list of ingredients as long as your leg, partly because fresh fish taste better than herbs and spices, and need no fancy French sauces.

Because I believe that most anglers already know how to dress a fish, I have elected to put most of the blood-and-guts stuff in the back of the book (Appendix I) along with tips on keeping and freezing the catch. This approach, although unusual for a book of this sort, will permit us to cook fish in chapter 1 instead of bogging down in skinning and scaling details.

I can only hope that the reader finds *The Freshwater Fish Cookbook* to be informative, instructive, mouth-watering, eminently browsable, inspiring, and highly entertaining. Of course, I know that all this is asking far too much of my limited ability to communicate my enthusiasm for the subject—but one thing I can say with absolute certainty: I sure enjoyed writing the book.

Good fishing—and good eating.

Easy Bass Creole (p. 2)

Black Bass

Largemouth, Smallmouth, Spots, Redeyes, and Blue-Bellies

Owing to its voracious feeding habits, the largemouth bass has long been the most popular warm-water sport fish in the American south. In recent years, bass tournaments and television fishing shows have helped spread the fever, and the proliferation of large man-made hydroelectric impoundments, recreation and flood-control lakes, and thousands of farm ponds scattered across the land have greatly expanded ideal largemouth habitat. The largemouth also thrives in most warm-water small streams and beaver ponds, as well as in brackish water. It has now been stocked in every state except Alaska. California and Texas are now largemouth hot spots, rivaling Florida, and both Mexico and Cuba are noted for very large bass.

The smallmouth bass is also a truly great sport fish, but it doesn't get large as the largemouth, and, unfortunately, its habitat and suitable spawning areas are much more limited. This species is popular mostly in the Northeast, the upper Midwest, and parts of Kentucky, Tennessee, and North Alabama, where some big ones grow.

Both the largemouth and smallmouth are black bass, a family that also includes the spotted bass (or Kentucky bass), redeyes, and various subspecies such as Chipola bass, Neosho smallmouth, Flint River bass, and others. (There is much confusion in the names of bass from one region to another, and not even an act of Congress could force the people of Kentucky to stop calling the spotted bass "Kentucky bass.") The smallest and perhaps the most unusual member of the black bass family, the Suwannee bass, lives only in certain clear-water streams in north Florida. It's a midstream fish—and it has, oddly, a blue belly.

The striped bass, white bass, hybrid bass, rock bass, and yellow bass are not black bass. These are covered in other chapters.

All of the black bass make excellent eating and can be cooked in a variety of ways. Some anglers will argue rather hotly that the smallmouth is better for eating purposes than the largemouth. Nothing I say here will change their minds, but I think that the main difference in all these fish is a matter of size. The small ones are more suitable for frying whereas the large ones are better for baking. In fact, an 8-pound largemouth is perfect for one of my favorite fish dishes—our first recipe.

Bass Veracruz

Mexico is a modern hot spot for trophy bass, and getting an 8-pounder for this recipe is not much of a problem. Scale and gut the fish, but leave the skin and head. The bigmouth's bucket head makes a good show on the table, gratifies the angler, and provides some tasty pickings for lunch the next day. If you think the eye socket might be off-putting to some of your guests, plug the hole with a pimiento-stuffed olive. The throat, a triangular cut between the gill plate and pectoral fins, is especially good.

Smaller bass, and larger ones, can be cooked by the same method by adjusting the cooking times a little. Several sorts of fresh peppers can be used in the recipe. I list jalapeños because they are widely available. They should be seeded and deveined unless you crave hot stuff and don't want to taste the fish.

- 1 bass, 6 to 8 pounds
- 2 medium to large onions, sliced
- 2 large tomatoes, sliced
- 4 fresh jalapeños
- 1 ½ cups dry wine
- ½ cup melted butter
- 1 lemon
- salt and black pepper to taste

Sprinkle the bass inside and out with salt and black pepper. Preheat the oven to 400 degrees. Use part of the butter to grease a baking pan large enough to hold the fish. Spread the remaining butter on the bottom of the pan. Layer the sliced peppers and top with onion slices. Place the fish on the onions and squeeze the juice of a lemon over all. Place the tomato slices on top of the bass, and pour in the wine. Grease a large sheet of heavy aluminum foil on the dull side with a little butter. Place the sheet, butter-side down, over the fish. Bake for 15 minutes.

Remove the foil and spoon some of the pan juices over the fish and tomatoes. Bake uncovered for another 15 minutes or a little longer. When done, the fish will flake easily when tested with a fork.

Using two spatulas, carefully transfer the fish to a heated serving platter. Top with all the tomatoes, onions, peppers, and drippings from the baking pan. Enjoy with rice, a green salad, and plenty of chewy bread.

Servings? A 6-pound fish will feed four to six people nicely. Leftovers are good the next day.

Easy Bass Creole

At one time, the bass was a popular market fish in Louisiana, where the species is often called "green trout" even today. A fish Creole can be complicated with a list of ingredients as long as your leg, but I have shortened this to a minimum by using chunky tomato-based salsa, now available in any supermarket. The salsa can be mild, medium, or hot, as you like it.

- green trout fillets
- chunky salsa
- shredded Monterey Jack cheese
- butter
- sea salt and freshly ground black pepper
- filé powder (optional)

Preheat the oven to 350 degrees. Melt a little butter in an oven-proof dish suitable for serving. Pyrex or Corningware will do. Add the fillets, turning them to coat all sides with butter. Sprinkle with salt and pepper. Top with salsa, slathering it out with a spatula. Sprinkle with shredded cheese.

Bake for 10 minutes, then preheat the broiler and broil close to the heat until the cheese is melted and starts to brown. Sprinkle lightly—very lightly—with filé powder and serve hot, along with rice and colorful vegetables of your choice. I like to cook this in a red au gratin dish, using one dish for each partaker.

A.D.'s Skillet-Fried Bass

I love to fry a few small bass (1-pounders) in my trusty cast-iron skillet. A deep-fryer works, of course, but I love the hands-on approach. I usually cook in the kitchen, not on the patio. Anyone who doesn't like the smell of frying fish, and thinks my method stinks up the house, can sit on the patio and enjoy the smell of insect repellent.

This method of cooking can, of course, also be applied in camp over an open fire. The trick here is heat control, which is best accomplished by removing the skillet from the coals whenever the cooking oil reaches the smoke point. A pair of heavy cooking gloves will help.

I usually scale the bass and cut it into bone-in serving pieces. Fillets also work, but it wastes a lot of good eating. When pan-dressing the fish (see Appendix I), be sure to save the throat, a triangular section between the pectoral fins and the gills. This is a choice morsel.

- small bass, pan-dressed
- stone-ground white cornmeal
- sea salt and freshly ground black pepper
- peanut oil for deep frying

Heat 1 inch of oil in a skillet. Salt and pepper the bass pieces and shake in a bag with the cornmeal. Set aside. On medium heat, cook the hush puppies and french fries first, draining them on a brown bag. Turn the heat up a notch and fry the fish last so that they will be hot for serving.

Serve the whole works on the brown bag, along with iced tea and a colorful salad.

Note: Every jackleg cook has a preference in cooking oils, breading, and so on, as well as in technique. Most people, for example, will want to cook the fish first, then follow with the hush puppies, saving the potatoes until last. Suit yourself. For a more detailed discussion on frying, see *The Quintessential Catfish*.

Sweet-and-Sour Bass

The Chinese cook wonderful sweet-and-sour dishes, and this recipe, calling for a whole fried fish, is usually made with sea bass weighing about 2 pounds. American black bass work just right. If you really want to pig out, as I often do, cook a whole bass for each person.

Whole fish are difficult to fry in most home kitchens, but the two-burner fish fryers, fueled with bottled gas, work just right on the patio. Beware that you'll need lots of oil, enough to cover the fish, but it can be strained and used again. I buy peanut oil in 5-gallon jugs, but I gallon will do for this recipe.

- 2 bass about 1 ½ or 2 pounds each
- peanut oil
- 2 slices of canned pineapple
- 2 carrots, sliced
- 3 green onions, chopped with part of tops
- ½ cup sugar
- ½ cup rice vinegar
- ½ cup pineapple juice
- ½ cup chicken stock
- salt and pepper to taste
- ½ green bell pepper, sliced
- ½ red bell pepper, sliced
- ½ cup flour
- 1 tablespoon cornstarch

Scale and draw the bass, leaving the heads on. Score the fish on both sides with 3 or 4 diagonal cuts about ½ inch deep.

Heat the oil in an oblong fryer to 350 degrees. While waiting, cut the pineapple slices into wedges and add to a saucepan with carrots, green onions, sugar, vinegar, pineapple juice, chicken stock, and a little salt and black pepper. Bring to a boil, reduce the heat to low, and simmer for 15 minutes. Add cornstarch. Cook and stir until the sauce thickens. Keep warm.

When the oil is ready, score the fish three times diagonally on both sides and sprinkle inside and out with salt and pepper. Roll the fish in flour to coat both sides. Lower the fish very, very carefully into the hot oil and fry until it is nicely browned on both sides. Carefully remove the fish, drain, and place them on a large serving platter.

Quickly heat the sauce almost to a boil. Stir in the cornstarch and add the bell peppers. Cook for 1 minute, stirring as you go. Pour the sauce over the fish and serve immediately. If you are adept with chopsticks, leave the fish in the middle of the table and eat it with chopsticks. If not, cut servings and put on individual plates, along with some of the sauce.

Fish 'n' Chips, the Livingston Way

Here's an easy dish that I like to cook in the oven. It's best to use a bag of thick-cut, wavy potato chips designed for dipping salsa. Remove about half the chips, leaving any pieces in the bag. Fold the bag and crush the remaining chips with a rolling pin. Shake the contents and roll again. Repeat until you have fine crumbs. For variations, try dill, Cajun, onion and sour cream, or other flavored potato chips.

- butter
- bass fillets
- potato chip crumbs
- salt and pepper to taste
- whole potato chips
- salsa and tartar sauce for dipping (optional)

Preheat the oven to 350 degrees. Melt some butter in a skillet. Roll the fillets in the butter, then roll them in the potato chip crumbs. Arrange the bass in a buttered baking dish of suitable size. Drizzle on some butter. Bake in the center of the over for 30 minutes. Serve with the whole chips, along with bowls of salsa or thick tartar sauce for dipping (recipe in chapter 16).

Black Bass Chowder for Yankees

In order to avoid rekindling the Civil War, let me say right off that an authentic New England fish chowder is a great culinary gift to the world. A lot of Yankee bass anglers, however, have been brought up believing that black bass taste muddy—and it's hard to get mud off the mind. I'm terribly sorry that Yankee bass taste muddy, but, if they really do, there's nothing I can do about it. Nevertheless, however, I submit that southern black bass is perfect for fish chowder. So, I'll slip in this short recipe for the world to enjoy while the Yankees are arguing amongst themselves about whether or not to allow tomato. I might add that I have support for my position by that great Yankee, L.L. Bean, who said in his early book on camping that black bass are choice for fish chowder. Of course, Bean probably had the smallmouth in mind, but, trust me, a Florida largemouth or a Kentucky spot works just as well, if not better.

For an old-time chowder made with white perch, see the New England Fish Chowder in chapter 10. For a lighter soup, see the Manhattan Fish Chowder.

southern bass fillets, halved
salt pork, diced
sliced potatoes
sliced onions
oyster crackers or chowder crackers
whole milk or half-and-half
fish stock or water
sea salt and freshly ground black pepper
no tomatoes

Fry the salt pork in a cast-iron Dutch oven until crisp. Drain and reserve. Add the onions, sliced potatoes, and bass. Almost cover with stock or water. Bring to a boil, reduce the heat to a simmer, and cook for 30 minutes. Add enough milk or half-and-half to cover. Simmer for another 20 minutes or so, but do not boil. Serve the chowder in wide soup plates, topping each serving to taste with salt and pepper. Sprinkle a few of the reserved cracklings on each serving. Float a few oyster crackers or chowder crackers on top, if you've got 'em. Serve with lots of chewy French bread for sopping.

B-BLT Sandwiches

Not many years ago, fish sandwiches were almost unheard of. But slowly they have found their way into restaurant menus—and they should be enjoyed more often at home, where some kids might turn up their noses at a large whole bass on the table. Skinless and boneless bass fillets work wonders in an ordinary bacon, lettuce, and tomato sandwich. I normally use only the tail-end part of the fillet from a large bass, saving the rest for other recipes.

If you want to use the oblong "loin" part of the fillet (the strip just above the rib cage) for making a "bassdog," see my recipe for Perch Dogs in chapter 10. Thus, one 6-pound bass will make two luscious sandwiches and two tasty bass dogs. It's great for the kids—especially if one of them caught the bass.

A lot of people use large round buns for fish sandwiches, but I really prefer thick-sliced white bread. Use two slices of tomato, cutting one in half and fitting the halves to cover the bread nicely.

1 bass fillet
3 strips of bacon
salt and pepper to taste
flour
2 slices sandwich bread
mayonnaise or tartar sauce (recipes in chapter 16)
2 slices of tomato
1 leaf of crisp lettuce

Fry the bacon in a skillet until it is quite crisp. Set aside to drain. Salt and pepper the bass fillet on both sides, dust it with flour, and sauté it in the bacon drippings over medium-high heat for 10 minutes, turning once. When done, it will flake easily when tested with a fork.

Slather both sides of the bread with mayonnaise or tartar sauce. Fit fillet on one slice, add the tomato, salt and pepper, lettuce, and bacon. (Use only one slice of bacon; too much will make the sandwich hard to eat, as will chewy bacon.) Cut the sandwich in half diagonally. Go ahead. Take a bite right out of the middle.

Chunky Black Bass Soup

Here's an impromptu dish that I cook from time to time, varying the ingredients as I go. The two essential ingredients are skinless bass fillets and cream of mushroom soup. The other stuff is optional, and can be varied according to what's at hand. It's a filling dish that hits the spot in camp, or for a shore lunch on a cold day.

For the peppers, I prefer jalapeños ripened to the red stage. Red bell peppers or cherry peppers can also be used.

- skinless bass fillets
- scallions
- red potato
- fresh red peppers, seeded
- butter
- Campbell's Cream of Mushroom Soup
- red wine
- freshly ground black pepper

Finely chop the scallions with part of green tops, a red potato, and the seeded fresh peppers. Melt a little butter in a skillet and sauté the vegetables until tender. Put the soup in a pan and turn on the heat to medium. Swish a little wine about in the can to clean it out, then pour into the pan. Stir constantly with a wooden spoon until it starts to bubble. Cut the bass fillets into bite-sized chunks and add to the soup. Stir in the skillet contents and cook for about 10 minutes, stirring as you go with a wooden spoon.

Ladle into a soup bowl. Sprinkle with freshly ground black pepper to taste. Serve hot with plenty of crusty white bread for sopping. Enjoy.

This recipe feeds two ordinary people, or one hungry angler.

Easy Broiled Bass

- bass fillet
- hollandaise sauce
- paprika (to taste)

Preheat the broiler and a greased broiling pan. Put a bass fillet, skin-side down, into the hot broiling pan. Slather generously with hollandaise sauce (recipe in chapter 16). Broil for 10 minutes, or until the bass flakes easily. (Note that the fish does not have to be turned, as the hot pan will help cook the bottom.) Sprinkle with mild paprika and serve hot.

A.D.'s Two-Skillet Bass Omelet

This dish, suitable for breakfast or a light lunch, can be made with leftover flaked fish, but I think it's best to start from scratch. If you are starting with fresh fish instead of leftovers, cube and dice a boneless fillet into ¼-inch squares.

Some people like their omelet to be light and fluffy, sometimes made with eggs beaten to a froth, but I want mine heavy and filling. Suit yourself. Consider this recipe to be for one omelet—and I allow a whole omelet for each partaker. If you or your guests aren't very hungry, it's easy to cut one in half. Note that most omelets are folded over half-moon style, but I usually make mine in the French manner, in which the sides of the omelet are folded over the middle.

4 scallions with half the green tops
¼ red bell pepper
¼ medium Roma tomato
2 strips bacon
½ cup cubed bass
3 chicken eggs
butter
salt and black pepper to taste

Dice all the vegetables. Fry the bacon in a small skillet until crisp. Remove and drain on a paper towel. In the drippings sauté the scallions and red pepper until tender. Add the fish and cook for 5 minutes. Add the tomato and heat through. Take off the heat.

Lightly whisk the eggs together, adding a little water to help break them down. In a second skillet or omelet pan, melt a little butter. Pour in the eggs. Cook on low heat until the bottom starts to set. Using a tablespoon, break up the bottom here and there, letting some of the uncooked egg touch the bottom. Continue until the egg is almost done. (Note that no turning is required.)

Add a row of sautéed vegetables in the middle from one side to the other. Sprinkle on the bacon bits. Carefully, use your spatula to fold one side of the omelet over the middle. Then fold the other side, lapping in the middle. Sprinkle with salt and freshly ground black pepper and serve hot. I'll take two pieces of that buttered toast and a glass of cold V-8 juice with my omelet.

Sautéed Bass Fillets, with Confessions

Don't tell my bass fishing buddies or the Florida Crackers in my neck of the woods, but I am quite fond of sautéing skinless fillets in a skillet with a small amount of butter and bacon drippings. Here's how.

Use no cornmeal or other dusting or batter. Heat the skillet on medium heat, then add the butter and bacon drippings. Sauté the fillets skin-side down for a few minutes, turn carefully, and sauté the other side until the meat flakes easily when tested with a fork. (Note that the surface of the fish should not be crispy or browned like breaded fillets cooked at high heat.)

Plate the fillets over a bed of rice and sprinkle lightly with salt and pepper. Quickly pour out most of the pan grease. Stir up the grimilles (little brown bits) with a wooden spoon and deglaze with a little water or wine. Pour the pan sauce over the fish and rice. Drizzle on a little freshly squeezed lemon juice. Serve immediately with white bread and vegetables or salad of your choice.

If you've got prissified guests for dinner, uncork a fresh bottle of wine, let it breathe a while, and, lying like a Texan, tell the company they are about to feast on Dover sole with Sauce Alfred Delano. Cross your fingers, lower your head, and pay homage to the great French chef, culinary writer, and snooty champion of the Dover sole, Auguste Escoffier.

Chipola Bass

A species of redeye bass that feeds heavily on insects lives in the Chipola River of Northwest Florida. Along the banks of the river grow several kinds of wild grapes, including the large muscadine. The Cherokee Indians built large arbors for these wild grapes, and early homesteads had arbors, many of which still exist. Muscadine and scuppernong grapes are now raised commercially, and are available in some supermarkets. The angler after a Chipola bass in late August can gather his own from along the stream. Be warned, however, that large red wasps like to build their paper nests in muscadine vines, so be prepared to get your ass wet.

Also see the recipe for Cherokee Mary's Smoky Mountain Trout in chapter 2.

- redeye bass, 1 to 2 pounds
- muscadine or scuppernong grapes
- butter
- salt and pepper to taste

Build a good campfire to dry your clothes. When it burns down to nice coals, dress the fish and stuff it with muscadines (or scuppernongs) and a pat of butter. Fold the aluminum foil all around, then make a fold in the fold to seal the package. Punch a small air vent in the top. Place the package directly onto the hot coals.

After 5 minutes, carefully turn the package to baste the top. After another 5 minutes, remove the package, unfold the foil, and test for doneness. If the flesh doesn't flake easily when tested with a fork, curse the author, reseal, and cook a little longer. Enjoy.

Trout

Brookies, Browns, Goldens, Rainbows, and Other Colorful Trout, with a Nod to the Bluebacks

I'll be lucky to get out of this chapter alive. Half the trout anglers in the land, a militant bunch, will want to shoot anyone who dares advocate the keeping and eating of a native American brook trout instead of releasing it back to the wild. The other half will want to skin any writer who doesn't champion the culinary merits of the world's best fish.

What's a poor writer to do? Vow to keep the preamble short, put on a bullet-proof vest, lower his head, and forge straight ahead, perhaps taking a shot or two myself to left and right.

Still, at the risk of having my name struck from the Orvis mailing list, I'll have to say that wild trout are not as important as either table fare or sport fish as the literature would have us believe. Owing to its limited and shrinking habitat, the stream-run wild trout is for the most part an armchair fish, as compared to black bass, walleye, and other species whose habitat has increased, often at the expense of trout streams.

Sure, we have highly regulated wild trout fishing still available here and there, and the angler can enjoy what I call subsidized fishing, making use of hatchery trout released into the wild and pay-for-fishing streams and ponds. Personally, I suffer no pangs of conscience whatsoever over catching and eating put-and-take trout. Somebody is going to do so.

To avoid further slings and arrows, I have arranged the brief listing below alphabetically, not on culinary preference.

Brown Trout. Native to Europe, the brown trout has been successfully stocked in North America, South America, Africa, and New Zealand. It is a wary target for anglers, and was probably the bounty behind the development of fly fishing in Macedonia. The brown trout is an excellent table fish, and is now farmed commercially for the masses and for hungry anglers who were not able to successfully match the hatch. A subspecies in Turkey was once called Allah Balik—"God's fish."

Char. This group of salmonoids includes the lake trout, the brook trout, the Dolly Varden, and others, as well as the arctic char. The difference between a trout and a char is determined by the fish's mouth structure, and taxonomists argue amongst themselves over what's what. The arctic char, as the name suggests, is caught in Canada, Alaska, and, to some extent in Maine. Some are landlocked and some are sea-run. They make excellent table fare, with flesh ranging from pale yellow to red. In Iceland, I understand, arctic char are smoked for the market over a smoldering fire made of dry sheep dung.

Cutthroat Trout. Various sub-species of the cutthroat are native to the West Coast from Alaska to northern California. They are found in lakes as well as rivers, and the anadromous species enters salt water. The cutthroat usually makes excellent table fare,

Macedonian Trout (p.15)

and its flesh can vary in color from white to red. It can be cooked a variety of ways, including smoking.

Dolly Varden. This species, a char, ranges from California and across the Northern Pacific. It has a rather oily flesh, making it ideal for grilling, broiling, and smoking. It is named for a character in a Charles Dickens novel who sported a pink spotted dress.

Golden Trout. One of the most beautiful fish that swims, the golden trout was originally restricted to the headwaters of the Kern River in California, but it has been been stocked in Wyoming, Idaho, and Washington. Generally, it is a high-altitude fish, growing in lakes as well as streams. It ranks very high as a food fish—if it is cooked soon after the catch. Its firm flesh is a little oily and doesn't keep well. Note that the Mexican golden trout is a separate species that lives only in parts of Mexico.

Grayling. These trout-like fish can be taken on dainty trout flies in the north country, mostly Canada, Alaska, and Siberia. Oddly, the flesh of the American grayling smells strongly of thyme (which accounts for its scientific name, Thumallus thymalluus.) The grayling makes excellent table fare, especially if you like the smell of thyme.

Hybrid Trout. As if piscatory classification isn't already complicated enough, biologists have developed several hybrid species for one reason or another, and this sort of species tinkering is certain to continue into the future, for better or worse. The last time I looked into this matter, a hybrid brook trout and lake trout is called a splake. Why? The "sp" part of the name came about because the brook trout is called speckled trout in Canada. The trousal is a cross between a brown trout and an Atlantic salmon. A tiger trout is a cross between a male brown trout and a female brook trout. A cutbow, of course, is a cross between a cutthroat and a rainbow. A brownbow is a cross between a female brown trout and a male rainbow. A sambow is a cross between an Atlantic salmon and a rainbow trout.

Personally, I would like to see more effort put into habit improvement instead of species adaptation. So, now I've also got the fishery biologists after me. Owing to limitations of space, I won't use the stocking of the carp or, more recently, the grass carp to mount a self-defense here.

Lake Trout. Sometimes called togue in the Northeast and mackinaw in the West, this large char (weighing up to 100 pounds) lives mostly in cold, deep lakes. It is usually caught by trolling. Having an oily flesh, it is more suitable for broiling, grilling, and smoking. Or roasting.

Rainbow Trout. Native to North America, this popular fish has been stocked in various parts of the world, including New Zealand. When migrating, the rainbow is known as the steelhead. The fish has a mild flesh that can be cooked by any method. It is now farmed on a commercial scale—but wild trout make better eating, giving the angler a culinary advantage once again.

Sea Trout. This is the anadromous form of the brown trout. Several saltwater species are also called sea trout.

Steelhead. See Rainbow Trout, above.

Others. A number of other trout species exist, but they are usually very, very localized. The sunapee, for example, lives in Sunapee Lake in New Hampshire. The Gila is native to the Gila River in New Mexico and Arizona, along with the Apache trout. The blueback trout exists only in a few lakes in Maine.

Some saltwater fish are called trout. These include speckled sea trout (or specs) and weakfish. Similar saltwater species include silver sea trout, sand sea trout, white sea trout, spotted trout, and so on. For the most part, these are members of the drum family.

Also, the term "trout" is applied locally to other species of fish. In the South, the black bass was often called trout or green trout until quite recently, and the cypress trout was the infamous bowfin.

Moreover, there is a problem with culinary classifications. Most anglers and honest men will agree that a wild fish makes the best eating. Hatchery trout dumped into our lakes and streams might be a necessity to keep the weekend anglers happy, but they tend to weaken the wild fish from a biological point of view, and, purists will point out, don't taste as good. Of course, farmed trout may be necessary to feed the masses, but, once again, the angler knows that wild trout make better eating.

Anyhow, most trout of similar size can be substituted for each other in the following recipes.

Trout Hemingway

Writer Ernest Hemingway was an avid fly fisher—and an unabashed trout eater. He started his writing career with a column in the *Toronto Star* newspaper, where the following recipe was first published along with notes on how to cook in a campfire (always on coals, not over the flame). The young Hemingway added that in a lifetime devoted "largely and studiously" to eating, he had never found a better combination. He used Crisco shortening, which (he said) was as good as lard for cooking purposes.

- 4 small trout
- 8 slices bacon
- 1 cup cornmeal
- 1 cup shortening, cooking oil, or bacon drippings

If your trout are large or your skillet small, you'll have to cook the fish in more than one batch. First, cook the bacon until it is almost done. Remove to drain. Dust each trout with cornmeal. Heat the shortening in the bacon drippings. Add the trout in one or more batches and cook over medium-high heat for 5 minutes. Top each trout with two strips of the partly cooked bacon. Cook for another 10 or 15 minutes, or until the trout are done—but not too done.

Trout Bradford Angier

The author of *Gourmet Cooking for Free* and other similar books, Bradford Angier had firm opinions about the cooking of trout. Although he preferred to proceed without any breading whatsoever, he grudgingly allowed a light dusting with flour, adding that cornmeal has an "unpleasant toughening effect." He also cooked the liver, heart, and roe with the trout. So . . . tell your good wife to save these choice parts when she dresses your catch. (Ladies! Ladies! Hold your horses. I'm just joking. It's all in good fun, so please don't write nasty letters to my publisher.) Anyhow, Angier's method, adapted below, works with most species, from lake trout fillets to whole brookies.

- whole trout or fillets
- heart, liver, and roe from the fish
- butter
- sea salt
- lemon

Heat 1 stick of butter in a skillet until it starts to brown. Cook the fish on medium-low, along with the parts, turning once, until the flesh flakes easily when tested with a fork. If necessary, cook in several batches, adding more butter as needed. Carefully remove the fish and parts to a serving platter. Sprinkle with sea salt to taste and drizzle lightly with lemon juice. Serve immediately.

Trout Herter

George Leonard Herter, associated with the large outdoor gear mail-order fame of yesteryear and author of an outlandish book called *Bull Cook and Authentic Historical Recipes and Practices,* pan-fried trout much like Hemingway and Angier—but he insisted on using a mixture of butter and beef suet, a fat that takes high heat without burning. Like lard, beef suet is hard to find these days. It is the solid white fat around the kidneys and loins. The very name of the stuff causes cholesterol nightmares these days—but it sure is tasty!

Trout au Bleu

Here's a dish that that my mother-in-law, God rest her soul, could not have prepared successfully. Anytime I brought home good wild fish and dressed them for cooking, she would scrub all of the flavor out of them—and then fry them until they were untoothsome. In any case, the success of Truite au Bleu, as the French call it, depends on having freshly dispatched trout with a minimum of handling. If the skin is washed too much, the blue will be lost.

I've seen lots of recipes for trout au bleu. Many of these are quite prissified, calling for court bouillon, vermouth, tarragon, and so on. The late James Beard cut through all this, as he had a way of doing, and set forth a simple version, saying that the fish is best prepared beside a stream from which it was caught. Beard was right, of course, and once again the angler has the best of the eating, with a minimum of trouble.

Heat 1 quart creek water to the boil. Add 1 tablespoon salt and 1 cup of vinegar. Bring the fish alive to the cook site, dispatch it with a blow to the head. Scale it, draw, and rinse in creek water. Gently dry the fish and carefully plunge it into the boiling water. Bring to a new boil, then remove the pan from the heat and simmer for 9 or 10 minutes, or until the fish flakes easily when tested with a fork. If all has gone well, the skin of the fish will have turned blue.

Put the trout on a serving platter and slather with a good hollandaise sauce. Serve with boiled new potatoes that have been slightly browned in butter and sprinkled with chopped fresh parsley.

Scotch Trout

The previous recipe notwithstanding, many anglers will prefer to dust their trout with flour or meal and fry as usual. Here's an interesting variation to try.

small whole trout or fillets
milk
oil for deep frying
salt and pepper
oatmeal
lemon

Gut the trout, put it in a bowl, cover with milk, and set aside for a while. When you are ready to cook, drain the trout and sprinkle inside and out with a little salt and freshly ground black pepper. Rig for deep-frying at 375 degrees, or heat about an inch of oil in a skillet. Zap some oatmeal in a food processor or blender until you have a fine meal. Roll the trout in the fine oatmeal. Fry for a few minutes, until golden brown on both sides. Serve with lemon wedges.

Macedonian Trout

Fly fishing for trout probably originated on a stream in Macadonia, where the brown trout once thrived. In this recipe, be sure to use Greek or Mediterranean oregano. (Mexican oregano is quite strong and can easily overpower mild fish. Oregano freaks should also see the recipe for Corfiot-Style Grilled Stripers in chapter 5, in which the dried blossom of the plant is used instead of the leaves on the Greek Island of Corfu.)

2 whole trout
good olive oil
sea salt
garlic to taste
1 lemon
Greek oregano

Preheat the oven to 350 degrees. While waiting, score both sides of each trout several times on the diagonal. Grease a suitable baking pan with olive oil. Roll the fish in the oil to coat all sides and sprinkle lightly with sea salt. Using a press, squeeze a clove or two of garlic over the fish and sprinkle very lightly with oregano. Top each fish with thin slices of lemon. Bake in the center of the oven for about 25 minutes. Garnish with a little fresh green parsley to go with the yellow lemon. Enjoy.

Peruvian Trout

Here's a tasty dish from Peru, where trout fishing is quite productive. It is made with queso fresco, a white cheese. It is sometimes available in Latino markets. If not available, use feta, as listed in the ingredients. I allow a whole small trout for each person.

trout
boiled ham, julienned
feta cheese, julienned
2 tablespoons flour
1 chicken egg, whisked
¼ cup dry bread crumbs
peanut oil
salt and black pepper to taste

Dress the fish head on with a small body cavity. Stuff with the ham and cheese strips. Dust with flour, roll it in the egg, and coat it with the bread crumbs. Heat about an inch of oil in a large skillet to about 350 degrees. Fry for 5 or 6 minutes on either side, turning once. Serve with fried plantain, wild mushrooms, and other vegetables or salad of your choice. Also try potato salad, remembering that the potato was first cultivated in Peru.

Trout Bercy, My Way

A bercy sauce, if you follow classic French cookbooks, is made with velouté, fish stock, and other ingredients. Before you can make it, of course, you have to make the velouté. This, according to my old copy of *The Escoffier Cook Book,* will require 1 pound of pale roux and 5 quarts of white veal stock. This in turn will require 8 pounds of veal or two uncooked fowls' skeletons, 2 ounces carrots, 6 ounces of onions stuck with cloves, 4 ounces leeks, a stalk of celery, 1 ounce parsley, 1 bay leaf, and a sprig of thyme. Well, to hell with it. We'll use a simple fish stock and a few other ingredients, requiring only one reference instead of hopscotching all over the book.

- 4 small trout, about 10 inches long
- sea salt and white pepper to taste
- 1 cup fish stock
- 1 cup dry white wine
- ½ cup melted butter
- ½ cup chopped shallots

Sprinkle the trout inside and out with a little salt and white pepper. Boil the fish stock and wine in a saucepan until it is reduced by half. Preheat the oven to 325 degrees. Grease with a little butter a baking pan or dish just large enough to hold the trout and add the chopped shallots, spreading out evenly. Arrange the trout over the shallots and pour in the fish stock mixture. Bake for 20 minutes. Serve hot with asparagus spears and a salad, along with some good bread and the rest of the white wine.

Pueblo Trout

Here's a recipe from New Mexico, where trout fishing is available on some of the Indian reservations. (The unsung Apache trout is native to the area and would be excellent in this recipe—except for one thing. The rather fussy Apaches of yesteryear were not too keen on eating fish or birds, including the turkey, that fed mostly on worms and insects.)

- 3- or 4-pound trout
- ½ cup freshly squeezed lemon juice
- 2 cloves garlic, minced
- 1 tablespoon red pepper flakes
- 1 teaspoon sea salt
- 1 scant teaspoon dried Mexican oregano

Mix all the ingredients except the fish in a bowl and let sit for 30 minutes to allow the flavors to mingle. While waiting, scale and draw the fish, leaving the head and tail on. Rub the trout inside and out with the lemon mixture and let stand for 15 minutes or so.

Preheat the oven to 350 degrees. Wet a suitable piece of cheesecloth with the lemon mixture, then wrap the fish in it. Then wrap with aluminum foil. Bake in the center of the oven for an hour. Serve hot with warm soft corn tortillas.

Roasted Lake Trout

This recipe works for a laker of about 8 to 10 pounds. Cook it whole, head and all.

As a general rule, allow 20 minutes per inch of thickness, plus 10 minutes for the stuffing. The fish is done when it flakes easily. Personally, I like to cook mine until the bacon looks ready to eat.

Servings? I allow half a pound of fish per person. Remember that leftovers are good, and can be used in a number of recipes calling for fish flakes. You won't need a recipe to scramble some fish flakes and eggs together for a hearty breakfast.

- 8 to 10 pound trout
- juice of 1 lemon
- ¼ cup butter (divided)
- 1 medium to large onion, diced
- 1 rib celery, diced
- 2 ½ cups soft bread crumbs
- ½ cup sour cream
- zest of 1 lemon
- thin bacon
- salt and paprika

Preheat the oven to 400 degrees. Sprinkle about half the lemon juice over the fish and into the cavity. Heat a little butter in a skillet. Sauté the onions and celery for 5 or 6 minutes, stirring with a wooden spoon. Add the bread crumbs, sour cream, lemon zest, and some salt to taste.

Grease a baking pan with a strip of bacon. Put the fish into it. Stuff the fish loosely with the bread mixture. Wrap with a strip or two of bacon around the fish and fasten with round toothpicks or small skewers. Baste the fish nicely with a mixture of melted butter and lemon juice. Bake in the center of the oven for 30 or 40 minutes, basting from time to time with lemon butter sauce.

Caucasian Trout

Here's a wonderful recipe from the Caucasian Mountains, where trout and pomegranates have been enjoyed for thousands of years. Any good trout of suitable size will do. Pomegranates are available at American supermarkets in autumn, and I am fortunate enough to have a prolific tree in my backyard. Although pure pomegranate juice, as well as syrup, can be purchased, some of this stuff is cloudy, no doubt from crushing the whole fruit, rind, pulp, and seeds. The best juice should be clear and red, like grenadine.

- trout
- melted butter
- salt and freshly ground black pepper
- pomegranate juice
- whole pomegranate seeds (for garnish)

Rig for grilling directly over wood or charcoal coals. Scale the fish and slit the throat just behind the gills. Use a long spoon to remove the innards. Make three shallow cuts on either side of the fish.

Sprinkle inside and out with salt and pepper. Insert long skewers through the fish, starting at the mouth and coming out near the tail. Brush with melted butter and grill until the fish is cooked through, turning and basting with pomegranate juice from time to time. When done, remove the skewers, sliding the fish directly onto a heated serving platter. Garnish with pomegranate seeds.

Grilling tip: It's best to rig for grilling without a rack. Position the skewered fish directly over the coals, resting the skewer on either side of the fire box. This method will eliminate the sticking problem. It's easy to rig for this kind of grilling simply by stacking bricks on either side of the hot coals. If you use a regular grill with grate, consider using a fish-shaped grilling basket, which will eliminate the need for a skewer.

Trout Hobo

This meal-in-a-pouch recipe is for the patio cook, or for the camp cook who doesn't have a skillet or other cooking utensil at hand.

1 small whole trout or fillet
2 slices bacon
1 medium potato, sliced
1 medium onion, sliced
salt and pepper to taste
flour
1 tablespoon white wine Worcestershire sauce

Rig for grilling over direct heat on the patio, or for cooking in hot coals in camp. Tear off two sheets of heavy-duty aluminum foil. Place one sheet on a flat surface and put down one strip of bacon, lengthwise. Add a layer of potatoes and a layer of onions, using half of both.

Sprinkle the trout or fillet with salt, pepper, and a little flour. Place the trout or fillet on the layer of vegetables, then put a layer of onions and a layer of potatoes on top. Drizzle with the white wine Worcestershire sauce, if available. Top with the other strip of bacon.

Put the second sheet of aluminum foil on top and seal with the bottom sheet, making double folds all around. Place the package on the hot grill for 30 minutes, carefully turning once; or, in camp, place it directly on a bed of hot coals raked out of the main fire.

Carefully, carefully remove the package and let it cool a little. Slit the top, making a boat, and enjoy first the aroma and then the taste. Sop up all the juices with a little bread, if available.

Cherokee Mary's Smoky Mountain Trout

The American Indians made good use of fresh and dried corn shucks in their cooking. The shucks add a nice flavor to the dish, as fans of authentic hot tamales know. Fresh shucks from roasting ears work best, but dried ones (for sale in supermarkets these days) can be soaked in water to soften. In any case, this recipe is great for cooking at a campfire.

This dish can also be cooked at home, on the patio, in the kitchen oven, or at the hearth in the den. It's fun to "eat Indian," serving this dish with slices of those luscious Cherokee purple heirloom tomatoes and an old Cherokee favorite, succotash. Native wild edibles, such as ramps, Jerusalem artichokes, catbrier tips (Indian asparagus), and so on can also be used.

Build a good fire and let it burn down to coals. Pull back the shucks on a large ear of fresh corn, saving all the silks. Remove the corn but leave the shucks intact, connected on the big end. Place a trout inside the shucks. Sprinkle with salt and pepper. Add a pat of butter, broken into small pieces, along with the corn silks for flavor. Sprinkle with salt and pepper. Close the shucks and tie with wet cotton twine.

Place the package directly onto red hot coals. Cook for 5 minutes, then turn and cook for another 5 minutes. Enjoy. Of course, you can also roast some ears of fresh corn in the coals, or you can boil the ears in a little water until tender.

A.D.'s Sumac Trout

Although I claim bragging rights to this recipe, it has surely been used in times past and in the Middle East, where sumac is a popular spice. Syrian sumac is generally considered the best—but don't believe it.

Once again, the angler has the best of the eating simply because wild sumac of several species grow along most streams and lakes of North America. All of these have red tasty berries—the source of Indian lemonade. (Don't worry. Poison sumac is a different plant, similar to poison oak, and has less conspicuous little white berries.) The flavor of sumac (a malic acid) is outside the berry and is easily washed off. For this reason, it's best to pick your berries before the rain comes and to refrain from washing them before use. If you don't trust me about all this, buy some expensive sumac powder from your spice merchant and modify the recipe accordingly.

skillet-size trout
butter
fresh sumac berries
salt

Dress the trout, sprinkle with salt, and sauté in butter for a few minutes. Remove the trout to a serving platter or plate. Add a handful of fresh sumac berries, unwashed, to the skillet and swirl around. Taste. Add more berries if needed. Strain out the berries and pour the sauce over the fish. Enjoy.

If you want some Indian lemonade with your trout, boil some stream water to make it safe to drink. Add a handful of sumac berries. Stir and taste. When it is tart enough to suit you, sweeten with a little honey or sugar. Serve over ice, if available.

Trout with Verjuice

At one time, verjuice was a popular seasoning, especially in imperial Rome and medieval Europe. It is simply the juice from sour (unripe) grapes. These grow along many trout streams in summer, free for the picking. Also note that a popular seasoning in Afghanistan, ghooray angoor, is made from green grapes that have been sun dried and pulverized. It's easy enough to make your own from streamside grapes.

For more about cooking fish with grapes, see the Chipola Bass recipe in chapter 1 and Walleye Veronique in chapter 4.

1 skillet-size trout
salted butter and olive oil
wild chanterelles or morels (if available)
unripe grapes

Sauté the trout and mushrooms in a little salted butter and olive oil for a few minutes. Remove to a serving platter or plate. Rinse some unripe grapes and add them to the skillet. Mash these with a wooden spoon or a streamside rock of suitable shape and size. Taste. Add more grapes if a more sour sauce is desired. Strain the sauce and pour it over the trout and mushrooms.

Cold-Smoked Trout

A lot of us have small portable smokers at home, often heated by an electric eye, and some of us enjoy smoking in a large covered grill or a double-barrel unit. Anyone who has experience at this sort of thing won't have a problem. Beginners are advised to follow the directions that came with their smoker. Cold-smoking basics are covered in Appendix II. The adventurous may also want to take a look at my book *Cold-Smoking and Salt-Curing Meat, Fish, and Game*.

- several small trout
- 1 quart good water
- 1 cup salt
- soy sauce
- cooking oil or bacon drippings
- lemon-pepper seasoning salt
- hardwood chips for smoking

Scale, gut, and butterfly the trout, using the belly flab as a hinge. Mix the water and salt in a non-corrosive container and add a little soy sauce. Marinate the trout overnight. Drain the fish on a rack for 2 hours. Rig for cold-smoking. Brush the fish lightly on both sides with bacon drippings or cooking oil and sprinkle with lemon-pepper seasoning salt. Cold-smoke for 8 to 12 hours. This, truly, is the angler's greatest reward.

Hot-Smoked Trout

In this method of cooking, the fish are soaked in a brine cure for only a short time, as compared to cold-smoking. Every jackleg cook will have his own recipe, often with a list of ingredients as long as your leg. Here's what I consider to be the basics.

- trout fillets
- 1 quart water
- ¼ cup sea salt
- ½ tablespoon brown sugar
- 1 bay leaf, crushed

Mix the water, salt, brown sugar, and bay leaf. Marinate the fish for 3 hours (as compared with overnight for cold-smoking). Rig for hot-smoking at 250 degrees in your covered grill, using hardwood chips. The fire should be on one side of the grill. Place the fish on the other side, close the cover, and hot-smoke for 30 minutes or so, or until the fish is nicely colored and flakes easily when tested with a fork. Serve hot—or cold with a lemon wedge.

A.D.'s Double-Barrel-Smoked Trout

I like to smoke fish on a large barrel-covered grill with a smaller offset fire box. There are several models, but most have a small barrel fixed at the bottom of one of the ends of the large barrel. The smaller barrel is used as a fire box, controlled by air dampers. Rigging a remote-reading thermometer in the larger unit will help you regulate the heat.

For cold-smoking, I like to run an electric extension cord to the small box and use a hot plate with a 6-inch cast-iron skillet to hold wood chips. For chips, I almost always use freshly cut wood chunks (usually pecan) instead of expensive and dry store-bought chips or chunks.

Toward the end of the smoking period you can, if you like, build a charcoal fire in the smaller unit and finish off the fish directly over the heat—but I seldom bother with this because I feel comfortable with consuming uncooked fish—if they are very fresh when I start and if nobody fusses at me about piling on the salt cure.

If you are new at this, see the fundamentals of cold-smoking in Appendix II.

- 1 or more nice trout
- 2 cups brown sugar
- 2 cups table salt
- water (about 1 quart)

Scale, draw, and butterfly the trout, hinging it at the belly. Dissolve the sugar and salt in a quart of water. Pour over the trout in a suitable container. (A small ice chest will do.) Marinate overnight in a cool place.

The next morning, rig for cold-smoking with hickory, oak, apple, or other wood of your choice. When you get a good head of smoke coming from the small barrel, dry the fish and place them on the rack, skin-side down, of the large barrel. Cold-smoke for 6 to 8 hours. If you can't wait that long, finish off over direct heat in the small barrel, doing two or three fish at the time, if necessary. Or add some hot coals to the large barrel to finish off the whole batch.

Crucified Trout

Various schemes and recipes have been set forth for armchair campers and Boy Scouts for spreading a trout open and cooking it before a campfire. I don't recommend the "plank method" for campfire cooking, but there are other ways of spreading the fish, as discussed in the next chapter. In all those schemes, the success of the "recipe" depends more on the technique, the fire, and a little luck than on the ingredients. That said, let me add that my favorite recipe for this kind of cooking is really simple.

- 1 trout for each diner
- ½ cup melted butter
- 1 tablespoon Dijon mustard
- 1 tablespoon dark brown sugar
- 1 tablespoon mild chili powder or paprika

Butterfly the fish, hinging at the belly. Open it up spread-eagle and attach it skin-side-down to a plank or paddle (see the Planked Salmon in chapter 3), or fix it Indian style (see the Campfire Salmon). Build a nice fire and let it burn down to coals.

Slather the fish heavily with a mixture of butter, mustard, brown sugar, and chili powder. Angle the fish to the coals and cook for about 30 minutes, or until the fish flakes easily when tested with a fork. Note that one side of the butterfly will contain the backbones. These can be lifted out before serving the fish.

Salmon Steaks the Maine Way (p. 27)

Salmon

Campfire Salmon, Gravlax, Kedgeree, Gypsy Skillet Salmon, Eskimo Chips, and Other Surprises

When I was in the Navy during my teens, I spent three "summers" along the coasts of Newfoundland and Labrador. During this time I caught and consumed a sinful number of Atlantic salmon, partly because there wasn't much else to do. I have also eaten some fresh Pacific salmon of one sort or another, but, to tell the truth, in recent years, while living in the warmth of Florida, most of my salmon have been farm raised and purchased at the seafood counter at the supermarket. Believe me once again when I say that anglers can indeed catch a better fish than they can buy.

A simple top-ten culinary listing of the salmons would have to be complicated by a lot of hemming and hawing. As a rule, those salmon that make long runs upstream to spawn are better eating at the beginning of the journey than at the end. Also, the fat content of the salmon depends partly on water temperature and other factors. In general, however, the salmon is a rich, fatty fish that is best grilled, broiled, smoked, or poached. Deep-frying is not recommended, although they can be fried quickly in a little butter and bacon drippings. Do not overcook.

Anyhow, here is my take on some of the more popular salmons. For a deeper appreciation of these remarkable fish, the reader should make a study of culture of some Alaskan Indians and the natives of some of the northernmost Japanese islands, where the whole way of life depended on the salmon.

Atlantic Salmon. This great sport fish is found in the North Atlantic, from Cape Cod to Russia, and it has become landlocked in some areas. Its flesh is quite oily, making it excellent for grilling.

Chum Salmon. This is a Pacific species that ranges from California to Japan, and it has become established all the way to Norway. It has a high oil content and is usually better for grilling or smoking.

Coho Salmon. Having a medium oil content, this excellent fish can be cooked by most any method and is especially good for smoking. (For frying, fry cut the fillets into fingers.) The coho's natural range is in the Pacific Northwest, but it has been stocked successfully in the Great Lakes. It is also called silver salmon.

Kokanee Salmon. This is a landlocked sockeye. The flesh is oily and does not keep well and should be iced down soon after it is caught. Do not fry or bake. The kokanee is sometimes called red salmon.

Pacific Salmon. This category comprises the chinook, the coho, the sockeye, the pink, the chum, and the cherry. The cherry salmon grows only in Asia.

Pink Salmon. This excellent food fish can be cooked by most any method. It is especially good when smoked, and, I will admit, the canned form, available in any supermarket, makes an excellent croquette.

Sockeye Salmon. Found from California to Japan, this fish with high oil content and excellent flavor is prized for smoking, grilling, or boiling.

I might add that some of the best eating is often wasted when salmon are merely filleted. The roe, white roe, liver, heads, frames, and other parts are excellent—and are readily available to the angler who catches his own. The American Indians of the Pacific Northwest made good use of the salmon and all its parts. Reportedly, they had over 80 recipes for the fish, and even the calcium-rich bones were ground down and used in the cookery.

Here are a few recipes to try.

Poached Whole Salmon

The hardest thing about poaching a whole salmon is finding a suitable container. A long poaching pan, suitable for using over two stove burners, is available commercially, but they are quite expensive and rather unpractical for home use. Try using a roaster or one of the long deep-fryers designed for two-burner camp stoves. If necessary, cut the fish in half, or behead it, and reassemble on the serving platter. Of course, a long serving platter can also be a problem. Rigging to poach a fish of about 4 pounds shouldn't be a problem, though.

You'll need quite a bit of court bouillon to poach a whole salmon. Use the recipe in chapter 16, or make some from scratch by filling the poaching pan half full of water and boiling some chopped celery, chopped onion, diced carrot, lemon slices, a couple of bay leaves, fresh thyme, salt, and pepper. Boil for 15 minutes, taste, and adjust the seasonings if needed. Add ½ cup dry white wine. Strain out the solids and keep the liquid simmering.

Dress the salmon, head on, and fold it in a sheet of cheese cloth. Twist the ends to make a handle and lower it into the boiling court bouillon. Turn up the heat until the liquid starts bubbling again. Reduce the heat and simmer for 30 minutes. Lift the salmon out by the ends of the cheesecloth. Partly unwrap and test with a fork. If it flakes easily, you're in business. If not, curse the author, rewrap the damn fish, and lower it back into the hot liquid for a few more minutes. Serve hot with a dill sauce or other condiment.

If you want to sauce this from scratch, dip half a cup of the used court bouillon into a saucepan. Add half a cup of half-and-half, 2 tablespoons melted butter, 2 chopped hard-boiled eggs, some chopped watercress or parsley, salt, and black pepper. Cook, stirring as you go, for a few minutes to reduce the stock. Serve over the poached salmon.

Planked Salmon

Unfortunately, cooking salmon on a plank is not practical for camp cookery, in spite of what some nostalgic writers and armchair campers have said. For one thing, where do you get a plank? One fellow suggested that you can hew one on the spot. Well, okay, but you've got to fell a tree in order to get a plank. Then you've got to have some nails and a hammer to fix the salmon fillet onto the plank. Another fellow said you can bore holes into the plank with a knife blade, then cut tapered pegs to secure the fish skin. After all that, you've got to make a set to hold the plank at an angle to the fire. Once you fix the plank, you'll have to unfix the hot plank to baste the fish or test for doneness. Then you'll have to reset it. Of course, you don't want the fillet to fall off the plank, and you don't want the whole works to topple into the fire. So . . . I have concluded that this method of cooking is not practical, although, I allow, it might well produce excellent results if successful.

If you want to try it, I suggest that you forget the whole plank concept. Instead, get some good 2-by-2s and nail or screw short segments of plank onto one end. The plank should be a little wider and a little longer than the fish or fillet. This method will simplify the setup considerably. I highly recommend that you use a cordless drill fitted with a 3-inch augur to drill a hole into the ground at a slight angle. This will allow you to insert and remove the planked fish easily. Make the set first, then build the fire where it is needed.

If you want to try the method, preferably in the backyard, have at it. You won't need a recipe, for the salmon, being oily, doesn't require any basting. If you are feeding modern foodies, however, be prepared to argue the matter at some length. Seems that plank cooking is something of a cult these days, and, of course, some sports hold firmly that alder planks taste better than oak.

But perhaps I am being facetious here, for most of the plank cookery is performed in an oven or in a large covered grill. This is a very old way of cooking and is still practical today for kitchen or patio. It is, of course, quite useful for cooking long fish that won't fit into everyday cookware. Anyhow, here's an old unprissified recipe, adapted here from *The Progressive Farmer's Cookbook.*

1 small salmon
¼ cup butter
mashed potatoes
2 or 3 cooked vegetables (carrots, English peas, cauliflower, etc.)
salt and pepper to taste
hardwood plank
mashed potatoes
lemon wedges (garnish)
fresh parsley sprigs (garnish)

Grease the plank with oil or bacon drippings and put it in the center of the oven. Preheat the oven, thereby heating the plank. When the oven is hot, brush the fish inside and out with melted butter and sprinkle with salt and pepper. Place the fish on the plank and bake for 35 or 40 minutes, or until the fish flakes easily when tested with a fork. (In general, allow 10 minutes per inch of fish thickness.) Carefully remove the plank from the oven and turn on the broiler.

Arrange a border of mashed potatoes around the fish (leaving room inside for the cooked vegetables), then place under the broiler for about 5 minutes to brown the potatoes slightly. (If you feel in a decorative mood, fill a pastry tube with the mashed potatoes and pipe a border of rosettes around the edge of the plank.) Remove from oven and arrange cooked vegetables around the fish. Serve on the plank, along with lemon wedges and parsley sprigs.

Campfire Salmon, Indian Style

The native Americans in the Pacific Northwest didn't try to hew a plank and nail a salmon to it. Instead, they cut a sapling, split it about halfway, inserted a butterflied salmon, pinned it open with several cross limbs, stuck it in the ground beside a fire, and cooked it until the fish was done.

This can be done at a single fire, preferably burned down to coals, or a number of sets can be made along a trench fire. The fish is fire-roasted first skin-side out, then turned 180 degrees and finished off.

Much ado is made in some quarters about the perfect staking angle for the fish, and some say to stake the fish tail down. It's best, I think, to angle the stake almost straight up. This will put the thick end closest to the fire. (Make the set before mounting the fish.) Note also that it helps to have a hole in the ground instead of pushing the stick in. This makes it easy to remove the pole if need be during cooking. A cordless electric drill rigged with a 3-inch augur bit is perfect for making the holes in the ground. So, be sure to try this in your backyard a few times. Then take the drill to camp with you if you've got room in the grub box.

Remember to use a straight sapling, preferably green, about 5 feet long. Slit it from the small end to a little more than halfway to the big end. Open it up and insert the fish with the center line on the sapling. Place a slender stake at the big end of the fish, crosswise, one in the middle, and one at the small end. The stakes should be a little longer than the butterflied fish is wide. Then the open end of the main stick is closed shut and secured with wire, cotton strings, or maybe a long twist-on. The end of the fish should be a foot or more from the end of the sapling, which will make handling easy. Also, the fish should be about a foot off the ground, so allow for the depth of the hole. All this can be worked out and eyeballed before you even build the fire. Have fun.

Before doing a whole salmon, you might want to practice this technique with a big mullet, shad, or other rather oily fish. A whitefish or a fatty lake trout 2 or 3 feet long will work. And remember that fatty salmon work best, so get them at the beginning of their spawning run.

To prepare for cooking, gut and behead a whole salmon. Cut the tail off. Starting at the big end, make a cut from the top, cutting through the rib and down to—but not through—the belly skin. Cut all the way to the tail end and butterfly the fish. Remove the innards, sprinkle with a little salt and pepper, and stake the fish as described above.

Fire-roast the fish for about 2 hours, skin-side out. If oil starts dripping out of the fish, the cooking is too fast. So, rake some of the coals away from the fire. When the fish is almost done, turn the stake 180 degrees and cook the skin side for 30 minutes or so, crisping it up nicely.

Chinook Steaks

Juniper berries have long been used as a spice or herb in Native American cookery, especially in the Pacific Northwest, as well as in parts of Northern Europe. Today they can be purchased at most supermarkets. If you don't have any at hand, however, simply brush the steaks lightly with a little gin, which is flavored with juniper berries.

salmon steaks (1 inch thick)
juniper berries (dried)
bacon drippings
salt

Build a good wood fire. While waiting for it to burn down to coals, sprinkle each steak with salt and stick on 6 juniper berries, spacing them out nicely. Rig a grid over the hot coals and brush it with bacon drippings. Also baste the salmon steaks on both sides. Grill for 6 minutes. Turn, baste, and grill for another 5 minutes. Do not overcook.

Salmon Dijon

Here's a quick and easy recipe for broiled salmon steaks or fillets. The fish should be 1 inch thick.

- 1 pound salmon steaks or fillets
- 1 tablespoon butter
- ¼ cup minced scallions with part of green tops
- 2 tablespoons good mayonnaise
- ¼ teaspoon lemon-pepper seasoning
- sea salt and white pepper to taste
- 2 tablespoons minced cilantro with roots
- ¼ cup white wine
- 1 tablespoon Dijon mustard
- 1 tablespoon honey

Preheat the broiler and arrange the rack close to the heat. Melt the butter in a skillet and sauté the onion for a few minutes, stirring as you go. Spread the onion over the bottom of a broiling pan or ovenproof dish. Mix the mayonnaise, lemon-pepper, sea salt, and white pepper. Spread over the fish. Broil for 5 minutes on each side (a little longer for thicker fish).

Sprinkle the fish with salt and white pepper, then carefully remove to a serving platter with a spatula. Pour the pan drippings into a small skillet, along with the wine. Reduce by about half, then stir in the mustard and cilantro. Stir for a minute, then pour the sauce over the fish. Serve hot.

Salmon Steaks the Maine Way

Here's a good one adapted from *The Maine Way*. The combination of butter, lemon juice, and Worcestershire sauce is great for patio, fireside in the den, or camp. The recipe can, of course, be cooked with either steaks or fillets. I prefer steaks for grilling, but suit yourself.

- salmon steaks
- 1 pound butter
- ½ cup freshly squeezed lemon juice
- ⅛ teaspoon Worcestershire sauce

Rig for grilling over hot coals, greasing the rack with oil or spraying with no-stick stuff. While waiting for the coals, melt the butter and mix in the lemon juice and "Wooster." When the coals are ready, dip the steaks in the butter mix and place on the hot grill. Grill for about 5 minutes on each side, basting from time to time.

The Maine Way says to serve this with hard-boiled eggs, cucumber slices, and lemon quarters. Suit yourself.

Salmon Steaks the Alaskan Way

Oil of eulachon, rendered from very fatty smelt, was once an important ingredient in coastal Alaskan cookery and candle making. (See chapter 12 for details on the eulachon.) The oil is still used, but these days it is in short supply and quite expensive. Bacon drippings or cooking oil will usually have to do for the lower 48.

See also the previous two recipes for grilled salmon. Remember too that fresh salmon makes for a good kabob. See the Whitefish Kabobs recipe in chapter 7 for the cooking method, and baste with melted butter flavored with crushed juniper berries.

- salmon steaks or fillets
- juniper berries
- eulachon oil (bacon drippings will do)
- sea salt and black pepper
- lemon wedges (garnish)

Using your mortar and pestle, crush some juniper berries. Press into both sides of each steak, along with a little salt and pepper. Set aside to let the flavors mingle. Rig for grilling over wood or charcoal, placing the rack about 6 inches above the coals. Coat the rack with oil to help prevent sticking. Also brush each steak on both sides lightly with oil. Grill for 5 or 6 minutes on each side, or until the fish flakes easily when tested with a fork. Serve with lemon wedges and homemade mayonnaise with a main meal.

Salmon Croquettes

This is one of my favorite ways to eat salmon. It can be made with canned salmon or, better, poached fresh salmon fillet.

- 1 pound cooked salmon
- 2 cups cracker crumbs (divided)
- 3 large chicken eggs, lightly beaten
- 1 medium to large onion, minced
- ¼ cup half-and-half
- 2 tablespoons butter
- 1 tablespoon minced fresh dill (optional)
- cooking oil for skillet frying
- salt and pepper to taste
- lemon wedges (garnish)

Flake the fish in a large bowl, removing any skin or bones if you are using canned salmon. Using your hands, mix in the beaten eggs, half-and-half, 1 cup of the cracker crumbs, onion, dill, salt, and pepper. Shape into oblong patties (about 2 by 3 inches will be fine). Roll the patties in the rest of the cracker crumbs. Refrigerate for about 30 minutes.

When you are ready to cook, heat about ½ inch of oil in a skillet. It should be quite hot, but not smoking. Fry the patties a few at a time for about 10 minutes, turning a time or two, or until they are golden brown all around.

Serve hot with a regular meal. Or, make them smaller and serve as finger food. No sauce will be required, but suit yourself.

Salmon Pancakes

I am fond of salmon croquettes and patties, but salmon pancakes are easier to make if you are feeding a crowd. A flat griddle works better than a skillet. Serve these for breakfast with bacon and toast.

- 1 cup cooked salmon flakes
- 2 chicken eggs
- 1 cup soft bread crumbs
- 1 tablespoon minced fresh parsley
- salt and pepper to taste
- half-and-half
- bacon drippings

Whisk the eggs. Add the bread crumbs, parsley, salt, and pepper. Mix in enough half-and-half to make a pancake batter. Heat the griddle and grease it heavily with bacon drippings. Add the batter in large spoonfuls to make a pancake, helping it spread a little with the spoon. Cook for a few minutes, turn, and cook the other side until well set.

Georgian-Style Salmon

Fresh salmon pairs nicely with tomatoes, a combination often overlooked in American cookery. Here's a recipe from the Republic of Georgia, adapted from *The Georgian Feast*.

- 2 pounds salmon fillet
- 1 cup good olive oil
- 1 large Vidalia onion (from the state of Georgia), sliced
- 1 large lemon, chopped
- 1 cup chopped cilantro (with part of roots if available)
- 4 bay leaves
- 4 medium vine-ripened tomatoes, sliced
- sea salt and freshly ground black pepper

Select a saucepan large enough to hold the fish fillets in a single layer with a minimum of overlapping. Add about ¼ cup of the olive oil, coating the bottom of the pan. Fit in the fish fillets (cut to fit if need be). Sprinkle on a little salt and pepper. Add the cilantro, onions, lemons, and bay leaves. Pour over all another ¼ cup of olive oil. Place the tomato slices on top. Pour on another ¼ cup olive oil and sprinkle with salt and pepper.

Cover the pot, bring to a boil, reduce the heat, cover, and simmer for 20 minutes, or until the fish flakes easily when tested with a fork. Serve with rice pilaf, fried eggplant, and a green salad.

Kedgeree

Here's a great way to use leftover cooked salmon. It's even better with smoked salmon.

- 2 cups flaked salmon
- 1 cup rice
- yolks of two hard-boiled eggs
- ¼ cup melted butter
- salt and pepper

Cook the rice in boiling water until tender. While waiting, flake the fish and chop the egg yolks. Melt the butter in the top of a double boiler. Mix the fish and rice. Stir into the butter. Sprinkle with salt and pepper to taste. Heat through, then top with chopped egg yolks. Serve hot.

Gravlax

Popular as an appetizer in Iceland and Sweden, gravlax is simply salt-cured Atlantic salmon eaten raw, usually with a mustard or dill sauce. Make it (or eat it) only with very fresh salmon. Note that you'll need two unpainted or untreated wooden planks to make the gravlax—and you need to clean off the bottom rack of the refrigerator before proceeding.

- 2 salmon fillets
- ¼ cup rather coarse sea salt
- 2 tablespoons sugar
- 1 tablespoon freshly ground black pepper
- 1 tablespoon finely crushed dried juniper berries
- fresh dill weed

Place the fillets skin-side down on a plank about 6 inches wide and a little longer than the fish. Mix the salt, pepper, sugar, and juniper berries. Sprinkle evenly over the fillets. Add a few sprigs of dill weed, evenly spaced. Carefully turn one fillet and place it on top of the other, making an even fit. Wrap the fillets with plastic wrap, overlapping all around. Then wrap in heavy freezer paper.

Put the package on a plank and tuck in the ends to seal. Place the second plank on top and press it down a little. Weight the top board with canned vegetables from one end to the other, or use another suitable weight of about 5 pounds. Put the whole works into the refrigerator for at least 2 days. Turn the unit over twice a day, but do not unwrap the fish until you are ready to eat. The gravlax should be eaten within 4 days. Slice paper-thin and serve as an appetizer on good dark bread with a mustard-dill sauce, such as the Mustard-Dill Sauce in chapter 16.

Creamed Salt Salmon

Soak a salt-salmon fillet, or part of a fillet, in milk overnight. When you are ready to cook, put the salmon into a shallow pan, cover with water, bring to a boil, reduce the heat, and simmer for 10 or 15 minutes. While waiting, heat some cream and butter in a saucepan. Drain the salmon and remove any skin and bones. Place on a serving platter and pour the butter and cream mixture over it. Serve hot with boiled new potatoes and sliced brandywine tomatoes.

Salmon Heads

Here's a short recipe from *The Alaskan Camp Cook*. The method works with other fish heads as well, so why not give it a try the next time you rig for deep-frying a batch of fillets. Anyhow, here is the entire recipe:

"Lay salmon heads upside down and cut through, taking out gills, eyes, and teeth. Fry."

Gypsy Skillet Salmon

Of Spanish origin, this old recipe, adapted here from the book *Gypsy Feast*, calls for juice of the sour Seville orange. If these are hard to find, substitute half regular orange juice and half lemon juice.

- 4 salmon steaks
- ½ cup Seville orange juice
- grated zest of 1 orange
- 2 tablespoons slivered almonds
- 2 tablespoons pine nuts
- 2 tablespoons raisins
- ½ tablespoon minced fresh parsley
- ½ tablespoon minced fresh marjoram
- ½ tablespoon minced fresh mint
- salt and freshly ground black pepper to taste
- water

Fit the salmon steaks into a large skillet. Mix the orange juice, water, salt, and pepper. Pour around the fish. Bring to a boil, reduce the heat to simmer, cover, and cook for 10 minutes. Turn the steaks and add the almonds, pine nuts, raisins, orange zest, parsley, marjoram, and mint. Cover and cook for another 10 minutes, or until the fish flakes easily when tested with a fork. Remove the steaks and reduce the skillet juices for use as a sauce. Serve hot, topping each steak with the sauce.

Soft Roe

Often called white roe, this is a great delicacy and should be more highly prized in American cookery. What is it? Well . . . it's a little too early in this book to reveal the secret, but culinary sports might want to flip over to chapter 15 for a discussion. Soft roe is very easy to fry, and is almost foolproof, and that's the way most people cook it. For a dozen ways of fixing it, see that French tome, *Larousse Gastronomique*.

- soft roe of salmon
- flour
- salt and white pepper
- cooking oil

Salt and pepper the soft roe. Dust with flour and set aside while you heat some cooking oil in a skillet. Fry the roe until nicely browned all over. Don't worry, cooking it a little too long won't be a problem. Serve hot, either as a side dish or along with vegetables, salad, and bread for a nutritious meal.

Salmon Caviar

I suppose that real caviar is made from sturgeon eggs, and purists will no doubt argue that the best comes from either the Black Sea or the Caspian Sea. Maybe so, but American sturgeon, salmon, and even carp provide good caviar—and, once again, the angler can have the best of the eating, and more peace of mind, by using very fresh roe. The fresher the better. If necessary, salmon roe sacs can be frozen in water until needed. Generally, the smaller salmon berries from coho make better caviar, and very large ones, such as those from the sow chinook.

It's easy to make your own caviar, especially if it is to be eaten right away. For directions, see the discussion for sturgeon and paddlefish in chapter 12. Meanwhile, here's a tasty and attractive snack made with red salmon caviar. (More elaborate creations include minced roast pheasant! So, use your imagination!)

very cold red caviar
very cold block of cream cheese
melba toast (or a good cracker)

Place the cream cheese on a small serving plate and top with red caviar. Each partaker uses a butter knife to spread some cream cheese and a few red berries over toast. Serve with very cold sparkling wine.

Note: I have made a similar appetizer with homemade yogurt cheese and small-berry caviar mixed and used as a spread.

Eskimo Chips

Every time I see skinless slabs of salmon in a fish market, I can't help but wonder what happened to the rest of the fish. The backbone, rib cage, tail, and head make a wonderful fish stock. In Alaska, steamed salmon bellies make a breakfast fit for company. The roe is good, as discussed above. The livers, often fried, have a delicate flavor and are exceptionally high in vitamin A.

It may come as a surprise to some persnickety people, but most fish skin tastes good when it is cooked until browned and crispy. Salmon skin makes excellent noshing fare, as enjoyed in parts of Alaska and in some of the northernmost Japanese islands.

Simply cut the skin into 1-inch squares and fry until crisp. Serve as an appetizer to a salmon feast.

Auke Bay Salmon Liver

Soak the salmon liver overnight in salted water. When you are ready to cook, slice the liver ½ inch thick. Sprinkle lightly with salt and black pepper. Set aside. Fry some bacon in a skillet until crisp. Drain. In the drippings, sauté some chopped onion until browned around the edges. Remove the onion and set aside. Add some butter to the drippings. Sauté the liver for a few minutes on both sides. Add the onions back to the skillet and heat through. Serve hot.

Sliced mushrooms can also be cooked like the onion and added to the fish. Serve with hash browns, sliced tomato, and hot coffee for a hearty lunch.

Patio Salmon Steaks

Salmon steaks work nicely on a charcoal or gas grill. Although this recipe calls for barbecue sauce (which is not usually recommended with fish), the jackleg cook can come up with dozens of bastes, and might even coin a recipe. Butter is the key.

- salmon steaks, 1-inch thick
- butter
- hickory flavored barbecue sauce
- salt and black pepper to taste

Rig for grilling. Grease the racks and place them from 3 to 4 inches from the heat. Baste the fillets with butter, sprinkle with salt and pepper, and place on the grill. Close the hood and cook for 7 minutes. Turn, baste with barbecue sauce, and cook for another 5 minutes, or until the fish flakes easily when tested with a fork. Serve with good baked beans, salad, and toasted garlic bread.

Milwaukee Walleye (p. 37)

Walleye and Sauger

Walleye Veronique, Hard Cider Sauger, Walleye Wellington, and Other Tasty Recipes for Minnesota's State Fish

Popular as a sport fish and as table fare in the upper Midwest, the Northeast, and parts of Canada, the walleye lives mostly in large lakes and streams, although it can survive in smaller waters. Impoundments in Kentucky and Tennessee also provide good fishing. The walleye is often taken by trolling, and with minnow-tipped jigs.

The walleye can grow up to 20 pounds. Its little brother, the sauger, weighs up to 3 or 4 pounds, although larger specimens are taken in the Missouri River impoundments. The average weight is about 1 pound.

The sauger almost always stays in big, deep lakes and impoundments, where the fish can roam in schools. They are often hard to locate, making the fishing a hit-or-miss proposition. Seasonal runs in fall and winter, however, provide some fantastic fishing in the tailwaters below large dams.

Both fish have mild white flesh, firm, tasty, and fine-grained. Although frying is a favorite way of cooking both walleye and sauger in mid-America, they can be cooked by any method. Here are a few of my favorites. For most recipes, I prefer to scale these fish, but many people will want to skin them. Suit yourself.

Walleye Veronique

Here's the perfect fish dish for a romantic candlelight dinner with a loved one. If you aren't courting, you might consider omitting the peeled red grapes.

2 pounds walleye fillets, skinned
1 cup seedless red grapes (optional)
5 or 6 scallions
½ cup fish broth or clam juice
¼ cup rosé wine
1 cup seedless green grapes
salt and pepper to taste
mild paprika

Peel the red grapes and set aside. Mince the scallions with about half of the green tops. Heat the fish broth or clam juice until it boils. Add the rosé and bring to a new boil. Add the fish fillets, reduce the heat, cover, and simmer for 5 minutes. Add the white grapes, scallions, salt, and pepper. Simmer for another 5 minutes, until the fish flakes easily when tested with a fork.

Using a spatula, arrange the fillets on a heated serving platter. Spoon the white grapes in the middle. Quickly reduce the skillet liquor by half and pour it over all. Sprinkle with mild paprika and arrange the uncooked red grapes around the edge.

Serve with French bread, steamed asparagus, and a colorful salad. Rosé wine marries perfectly with the red and white grapes.

Vietnamese Walleye

Fish sauce is a popular cooking ingredient, and table condiment, in Southeast Asia. Use it sparingly, for its strong flavor will really kick up a bland dish of fish.

1 pound walleye fillets
1 hot green chile
1 hot red chile (such as cherry pepper)
flour
water
3 tablespoons peanut oil (used twice)
Asian fish sauce
3 shallots, thinly sliced
4 medium tomatoes, chopped
2 teaspoons rice vinegar
black pepper (used twice)

Seed and devein the peppers, then finely chop them. Mix a paste with 1 tablespoon flour and 3 tablespoons water; set aside.

Heat 1 tablespoon of the oil in a skillet and lightly brown the fish fillets on both sides. Using a spatula, carefully remove the fillets to drain on a brown bag. Sprinkle both sides of each fillet with a little fish sauce, using a total of about 1 tablespoon.

Put 2 tablespoons of peanut oil into the skillet, then sauté the shallots and peppers for 5 minutes. Add the tomatoes, 2 tablespoons of fish sauce, and ½ cup water. Simmer for about 15 minutes. Add the flour paste and stir until the sauce thickens. Stir in the rice vinegar.

Carefully place the fillets back into the skillet and simmer for 3 or 4 minutes. Transfer the fish and pan sauce to a serving dish. Grind a little black pepper over each fillet and serve with rice and and a colorful salad. A bottle of fish sauce is usually put on the table for those who want it. (And I am an absolute addict.)

Milwaukee Walleye

Here's a popular recipe for Midwesterners, rednecks, and beer-drinkers everywhere.

2 pounds walleye fillets
1 cup Bisquick
½ teaspoon salt and pepper
1 can Miller Lite
3 cups cracker crumbs
3 chicken eggs
½ teaspoon salt and pepper

Rig for deep-frying at 375 degrees (see chapter 11 for tips on deep-frying). Mix the Bisquick, salt, and pepper in a bowl and stir in enough beer to make a batter. Dip the fish fillets in the batter, then roll in cracker crumbs. Set aside. Drink the rest of the beer while waiting for the oil to heat. Fry a few fillets at a time until nicely browned. Feeds four.

Poor Man's Lobster

Here's a recipe from Dan Gapen, Sr., writer and lure maker (Gapen's), son of Don Gapen, the inventor of the famous Muddler Minnow. I have adapted the recipe from Dan's book *Wildness North*.

4 pounds boneless walleye fillets, skinned
1 large onion, chopped
3 ribs celery with part of green tops, chopped
1 cup sherry
¾ pound butter, melted
½ cup freshly squeezed lemon juice
salt and paprika to taste

Cut the fillets into 2-inch chunks. Put about a gallon of water in a stockpot and bring to the boil. Preheat the broiler. Add the onion, celery, and lemon juice to the pot. Bring to a new boil, reduce the heat and simmer for 5 or 6 minutes. Add the fish and simmer for 5 or 6 minutes.

Drain the fish and place them in a large broiling pan, spreading out evenly. Brush with melted butter and sprinkle with salt and paprika. Broil close to the heat for 2 minutes. Turn the pieces with tongs, then brush again with butter and sprinkle with paprika. Broil for another 2 minutes.

Garnish with yellow lemon wedges for squeezing and green parsley for color. This makes nice buffet finger food for a crowd, and the price is right if you catch your own walleye. The chunks are easily eaten with round toothpicks, and my Lemon Butter recipe (chapter 16) makes a tasty dip.

Easy "Oven-Fried" Walleye Fillets

Here's one for honest folks and anglers who want a crispy fish without a lot of grease. But we all know it's not really fried.

6 or 8 small walleye fillets, about 1 inch thick
flour
salt and black pepper
1 stick of butter

Mix the flour, salt, and black pepper in a bag. Shake the fillets, one or two at a time, and set aside. Preheat the oven to 350 degrees. Melt the butter in a baking pan. Lay in the floured fillets and bake in the center of the oven for 15 or 20 minutes, or until the fish is nicely browned and flakes easily when tested with a fork.

Hard-Cider Sauger

Here's an old New England dish that can be cooked to perfection with fillets of either sauger or walleye. Use wild morels or chanterelles, if available. If necessary, button mushrooms from the supermarket will do.

1 pound sauger fillets
¼ pound mushrooms, sliced
1 cup hard cider
2 tablespoons butter
2 tablespoons flour
¼ cup grated hard cheese
salt and black pepper to taste

Preheat the oven to 350 degrees. Put the fillets in a well-greased baking dish suitable for serving. Top with mushrooms. Pour hard cider over all and sprinkle with salt and pepper. Bake in the middle of the oven for 20 minutes. Remove the dish from the oven and preheat the broiler.

In a small pan or skillet, melt the butter and stir in the flour. Cook and stir until you have a light roux. Add the liquid from the baked fish, cooking and stirring until you have a nice sauce. Pour the sauce over the fish. Sprinkle with grated cheese, and broil until lightly browned. Serve immediately.

Whole Fried Sauger

Here's a recipe for cooking fish for a crowd during the sauger run. You'll need an oblong fish fryer designed for cooking over a two-burner camp stove. Medium or small sauger, about 12 inches long, are perfect for this recipe.

Rig for deep-frying (with 3 or 4 inches of cooking oil) at 375 degrees. While the oil heats, scale, behead, and gut the fish. Score the sides of the fish three or four times on either side. Dip them one at a time in lightly beaten egg, then roll them in a mixture of yellow cornmeal, white flour, salt, and pepper. Fry in deep fat at 375 degrees for about 15 minutes, or until nicely browned. Drain the fish well on brown bags and serve with sliced tomatoes, french fries, and hush puppies.

Skillet Walleye with Roux

You'll need a wide skillet with a lid to cook this recipe, which calls for 2 walleye of about 3 pounds each. If you don't have one such a skillet, try an oblong fish cooker designed for a two-burner camp stove. Remove the heads and tails of the fish if necessary to make it fit.

- 2 walleye about 3 pounds each
- ½ pound salt pork, diced
- ¼ cup all-purpose flour
- 1 large onion, chopped
- 2 cups chopped tomatoes
- salt and black pepper to taste
- 2 stalks celery with green tops, chopped
- 1 green bell pepper, chopped

Sauté the salt pork until brown and crisp and most of the oil has fried out. Remove the cracklings to drain. Set aside—and don't let anybody eat them.

To make the roux, add the flour 1 tablespoon at the time to the skillet, stirring as you go. (You should have enough grease to absorb the flour. Add a little bacon drippings if needed.) Stirring constantly with a wooden spoon, cook on very low heat until the flour is browned or until your arm gets tired—the longer the better, provided that the flour doesn't burn. Add the onions and cook for another 5 minutes. Then stir in the tomatoes, celery, bell pepper, black pepper, and salt.

Increase the heat to high. Place the fish in the skillet, cover, decrease the heat to medium, and cook for 20 minutes without peeking. Remove the cover, turn the fish, recover, and cook for another 10 minutes, or until the fish flakes easily when tested with a fork. Carefully place the fish whole on a serving platter and spoon the skillet gravy over all. Serve hot.

Sprinkle the salt pork cracklings over the baked potato (topped with sour cream) or over the tossed salad.

Creamed Walleye

I don't know the history of this recipe, but I suspect that it is quite old. I adapted this version from a book of traditional Irish recipes, which called it creamed haddock, with a note saying it would be suitable for cooking any white fish, such as cod. I find it to be a delicious way to cook bass and walleye fillets. It's very rich and filling, especially if you use real butter instead of margarine.

- 1 pound walleye fillets, skinned
- 1 cup half-and-half
- ½ cup butter
- flour
- salt and pepper
- 1 teaspoon dry mustard
- fresh parsley

Skin the fillets, then sprinkle them with salt and pepper. Melt the butter in a small skillet or saucepan. Dip the fillets in the melted butter, then sprinkle them with flour. Place the fillets carefully in a large well-greased skillet. Mix the half-and-half into the melted butter, then pour the mix over the fillets. Heat the skillet until the liquid around the fillets starts to bubble. Reduce the heat immediately and simmer (do not boil) for about 10 minutes, or until the fish flakes easily when tested with a fork. (The exact time will depend on the thickness of the fillets and on the heat.) Carefully take up the fillets with a spatula and gently arrange them on a heated serving platter.

Mix the mustard into the liquid left in the large skillet. Heat until it starts to bubble, then reduce the heat and simmer until the sauce starts to thicken. Pour the sauce over the fish. Garnish with parsley and serve hot. I like this dish with new potatoes, snap beans, and canned pear halves stuffed with homemade mayonnaise and sprinkled with shredded cheddar cheese. If you're on a diet, however, you really ought to count the calories in all this.

Zesty Fillets

Here's a cooking method that I like to use with fillets, using both a griddle and a broiler. The process eliminates the need for turning broiled fish, which can tear them apart.

walleye or sauger
cooking oil and butter
Zesty Italian dressing

Preheat the broiler and heat the griddle on the stove burner. Grease the griddle to help prevent sticking. Sauté the fillets skin-side down until the bottom starts to brown. Remove the griddle from the stove top and place it in the broiler, about 4 inches from the heat. Baste with Zesty Italian dressing. Cook for a few minutes, basting once more. When the fish is done, carefully remove each fillet to a serving plate.

Walleye with Indian Rice

Since both walleye and wild rice are so popular in the upper Midwest, it seems fitting to put them together. I think a thick walnut sauce goes well with this dish, served over both fish and wild rice.

2 pounds walleye fillets
4 slices bacon, chopped
1 cup chopped mushrooms
½ cup minced onion
¼ cup finely chopped celery with green tops
2 cups cooked wild rice prepared by package directions
¼ cup butter
salt and pepper to taste
Walnut Sauce (recipe in chapter 16)

Preheat the oven to 350 degrees. Sauté the bacon in a skillet until browned. Add the mushrooms, onion, and celery. Sauté for 5 minutes, stirring a time or two and adding some salt and pepper to taste. Mix in the cooked wild rice. Grease a baking pan of suitable size and fit in the fillets. Spoon the wild rice mixture evenly over the fillets. Melt the butter and drizzle it on top. Bake in the center of the oven for 20 minutes. Spoon some of the walnut sauce over the dish and serve the rest at the table.

Corn-Belt Fish Chowder

I have decided to add this recipe from the Midwest under the name of "chowder," letting the rest of the country in on an outstanding dish. It should delight frugal souls everywhere. So, be sure to keep the heads and bony parts when you dress the walleyes. And save the cobs and silks with your shucked corn.

- 4 or 5 pounds walleye (undressed weight)
- 3 or 4 slices salt pork (or substitute bacon)
- very fresh roasting ears of corn
- 3 large potatoes
- 1 medium to large onion, diced
- 1 rib celery with green tops, diced
- 2 cups half-and-half
- water for "fish and corn" stock
- salt and freshly ground black pepper
- 2 bay leaves (optional)

Fillet the walleyes and set aside. Put the heads and backbones in a pot. Cover with water. Add the bay leaves and bring to heat. Shuck several ears of corn and cut off enough kernels to make 2 cups. Set aside. Scrape the cobs, as when making creamed corn. Set the pulp aside. Put the corn cobs, and the corn silks, into the pot with the fish. (These add to the flavor.) Boil slowly for an hour or so. Strain out 2 cups of the broth. Fish out the walleye heads and backbones. Flake off any remaining flesh and set aside, discarding bones.

In a stove-top Dutch oven, sauté the salt pork until most of the oil has been rendered. Drain the cracklings and set aside. Add the corn kernels, onions, and celery. Sauté until the onion starts to brown. Add the potatoes and corn scrapings. Cut the fillets into 1-inch chunks and add to the pot. Add 2 cups of the fish stock, along with salt and pepper to taste. Simmer, covered, for 20 minutes.

Add the half-and-half. Bring back to heat, stirring with a wooden spoon as you go, but do not boil. Taste and add a little more salt and pepper if needed. Serve hot in bowls, sprinkled with the reserved cracklings. Oyster or chowder crackers go nicely with this chowder, but a crusty French-type bread or homemade biscuit halves work better for sopping.

Minnesota Po' Boy

The walleye is available commercially in Minnesota and has been dubbed the state fish. Fried walleye was covered in *Roadfood Sandwiches* by Jane and Michael Stern, as made at Tavern on Grand in St. Paul. In this neck of the woods, yellow cornmeal is usually used for a dusting. I'll allow it here, but, really, white whole-kernel finely ground meal is better for frying. Suit yourself.

- 4 walleye fillets
- 1 cup yellow cornmeal
- 2 large chicken eggs, lightly beaten
- vegetable oil for frying
- 4 hero rolls
- butter for pan-grilling the rolls (optional)
- Tartar Sauce (chapter 16)
- shredded iceberg lettuce
- 1 large tomato, thinly sliced
- salt and pepper to taste

Mix some salt and pepper into the cornmeal and put into a shake bag. Flop the fillets in beaten egg and shake in the flour. Set aside. Heat an inch of cooking oil in a skillet to 375 degrees. Fry the fillets two at a time until nicely browned and have a crusty. (Note: I recommend cutting the fillets in half lengthwise before frying. This makes them easier to fit, side by side, into the hero bun, ends reversed.)

Butter the rolls lightly and grill them lightly in another skillet. Spread both sides of each roll generously with tartar sauce. Sprinkle shredded lettuce on the bottom roll. Top with a walleye fillet (or two halves). Close sandwich and cut in half lengthwise. Serve while still hot. I'll take mine with a spear of dill pickle and lots of thick potato chips.

Walleye Wellington

The fillets should weigh about ½ pound each, scaled and skinless. Larger or smaller fillets can also be used, as well as fillets from large crappie, smallmouth bass, and so on.

2 matching walleye fillets
juice of 1 medium lemon
crab stuffing (see below)
8-ounce can crescent rolls
1 chicken egg yolk
¼ teaspoon each salt and pepper

Crab Stuffing
½ pound flaked crabmeat
½ cup bread crumbs
½ cup chopped celery with green tops
⅓ cup whipping cream
¼ cup melted butter
1 teaspoon lemon-pepper seasoning salt
1 egg white
grated zest of 1 lemon

Sprinkle the fillets with lemon juice, then with salt and pepper. Set aside.

Preheat the oven to 450 degrees. Mix the stuffing in a bowl and set aside.

Remove the crescent roll dough and halve it. On a floured surface, roll out each half. Using the fillets as a guide, cut each dough sheet into two fish shapes, one about 1 inch larger than the other all around. Place the smaller fish shapes on a greased baking sheet. Put a fillet on each and spread the stuffing evenly. Top with the second fillet. Any remaining stuffing should be placed on top and around the sides, fitting it in snugly. Top with the larger sheet of fish-shaped dough and pinch the edges all around. If you are a food stylist or culinary artist, make fins, eyes, mouths, and gills with scraps of dough.

Brush the top with the egg mixed with a little water. Bake for 10 minutes. Decrease the heat to 350 degrees and cook for another 10 minutes, or until the crust is brown. Servings? I want a whole Wellington on my plate.

Striped Bass, White Bass, and Hybrids

Striper with Pasta à la Joe Dogs Lannuzzi, Bass à la Bonne Femme, Rockfish Wingo, and Other Recipes for Stripers and White Bass

Not many years ago, the striped bass was almost entirely an anadromous species, living mostly in coastal salt and brackish waters and ascending rivers in spring to spawn. It occurs on both coasts and in the Gulf of Mexico. More and more, landlocked stripers have become important in some of our large impoundments. Saltwater stripers grow to over 100 pounds, but landlocked fish seldom exceed 50 pounds.

Striped bass are often called rockfish, especially south of New Jersey. I prefer that name and use it fondly in some of the recipes below.

The white bass is a much smaller fish with similar schooling habits. It is popular in large lakes and impoundments from the Great Lakes to the Southwest. It is the state fish of Oklahoma, where sport fishers catch and hopefully eat a surprising 2.5 million pounds annually. The white bass runs small, averaging about a pound. It can grow up to 6 pounds, but this is quite rare.

Note that the white bass is often called white perch, further confusing the issue. Even some fish and game cookbooks, written by authors who ought to know better, confuse these fish. (Even worse, one outdoor writer set forth a "white perch" recipe calling for the fish, cherries, and cucumbers!) Anyhow, I have discussed the real white perch in a separate chapter, along with the yellow perch and others.

The hybrid bass is a cross between the striper and the white bass. These are hatched in captivity and released or stocked into selected streams and lakes. In Florida, the hybrid has been officially dubbed the Sunshine bass.

The yellow bass is a fish of mid-America, from southern Minnesota to the Tennessee River. It looks quite like a white bass, and is of about the same size or maybe a little smaller, running about half a pound. In spite of its small size, however, it might well be the best eating of this bass family.

All of these fish, however, make good table fare if they are properly handled after the catch. I recommend putting them on ice or in slush as soon as they are caught. The problem for the angler is to distinguish one fish from the other. Fish and game regulations often carry pictures of each, showing slight differences in spots and other features.

Filipino Fish Steaks (p. 47)

Joe Dogs' Striper with Pasta

Here's a dish cooked by Joseph "Joe Dogs" Lannuzzi, as described in *The Mafia Cookbook.* Joe Dogs specified ¼ pound of monkfish, but I use ½ pound of striper fillets. The striper has firm white flesh, and fingers of it are sometimes used as a substitute for shrimp. If you are a pasta fan as well as an angler, be sure to try this.

½ pound striper fillets
1 pound linguine
¼ cup extra-virgin olive oil
1 stick butter
½ cup flour
½ cup dry white wine
2 or 3 tablespoons finely minced garlic (Joe Dogs minced his with a single-edged razor blade!)
1 cup chopped fresh parsley
flour
sea salt and freshly ground black pepper to taste

Start the linguine cooking in 2 quarts of boiling water. (Do not overcook. It should be al dente.) Cut the fish into 1-inch chunks and shake in a bag with a little flour. Heat the olive oil in a skillet and sauté the fish until golden brown, stirring as you go with a wooden spoon. Add the garlic and wine. Simmer for 5 minutes.

Check on the pasta. When it is ready, drain it in a colander. Set aside.

Add the butter to the skillet. When it is melted, stir in the salt, pepper, and parsley.

Put the pasta on individual plates. Top equally with the fish chunks, and pour the pan sauce over all. Serve with a chewy bread. Feeds two mobsters or anglers, or four ordinary people.

Bass à la Bonne Femme

This French housewife dish works wonders for a striped or hybrid bass of 4 or 5 pounds. Scale and fillet the fish, saving the head and bony parts for fish stock (recipe in chapter 16). Allow ½ pound of fillets per person.

2 pounds bass fillets
1 cup chopped shallots
4 ounces sliced mushrooms
3 egg yolks
fish stock
white wine
butter
salt and pepper

Preheat the oven to 350 degrees. Butter the bottom of a baking pan and sprinkle evenly with the shallots. Lay in the fillets, skin-side down, and cover with sliced mushrooms. Sprinkle with salt and pepper. Pour in enough wine and fish stock, equal parts, to cover the bottom of the dish. Bake for 10 minutes, or until the fish flakes easily when tested with a fork.

Using two spatulas, carefully remove the fish to a heated serving platter. Quickly beat the egg yolks along with a little of the warm pan liquid. Stir the egg yolk and a little butter into the pan liquid to make a sauce. Pour the sauce over the fish and serve immediately.

Rockfish Wingo

Here's a recipe from a friend of mine who says it makes fish readily acceptable to his kids. The secret? He uses sugar-coated cornflakes, well crushed with a rolling pin. Of course, regular cornflakes can also be used for feeding adults.

striped bass fillets, skinless
cornflakes
chicken egg
salt and pepper to taste
peanut oil for frying

Cut the fillets crosswise into fingers and sprinkle lightly with salt and black pepper. Crush the cornflakes with a rolling pin, or zap them in a food processor. Whisk the egg in a bowl along with a little water. Roll the fillets first in the egg mixture and then in the cornflakes. Set aside.

Heat the oil in a skillet to 375 degrees. Fry a few bass fingers for 5 minutes or so, or until nicely browned and crisp. Drain and cook another batch. Serve hot with french fries and a salad.

Whole Fried White Bass

Schooling white bass often lead to a big catch of rather small fish. These are perfect for frying whole. I like to scale and gut them, leaving the head on, and make three diagonal cuts on either side. A skillet is not ideal for frying whole fish, but a deep skillet, sometimes called a "chicken fryer," will work. A two-burner rig, fitted with an oblong fryer, is ideal.

small white bass
fine cornmeal or flour
salt
oil for deep-frying

Rig for deep-frying, heating at least 3 inches of oil to 375 degrees. Salt the bass inside and out and dust all over with cornmeal or flour. When the oil is hot, fry the fish one or two at a time until golden brown. Drain and serve, giving each partaker a whole fish. If you are going to heat all that oil, you might as well fry some green tomatoes along with the hush puppies.

See also the Mock Shrimp recipe later in this chapter.

Broiled Striper Slabs

Here's an easy method for cooking rather large fillets from stripers or hybrids.

striper fillets
lemon
salt
mayonnaise
paprika

Drizzle the fillets with a little lemon juice and sprinkle with salt. Set aside. Place a large broiling pan or rack under the broiler heat source. Preheat the broiler and heat the pan. (This will help cook the fillets without having to turn them.) Spray the broiling pan with Pam (or use a little cooking oil) and carefully lay in the fillets skin-side down. Slather generously with mayonnaise.

Broil the fillets for about 10 minutes per inch of thickness, or until the the meat flakes easily with tested with a fork. Using two spatulas, carefully remove the fillets to a long serving platter. Sprinkle with paprika and garnish with lemon slices.

Outer Banks Muddle

Here's a recipe from coastal Carolina, where regular potatoes, as opposed to sweet potatoes, are called "Irish" potatoes. The recipe can be made with striped bass or hybrids, or large whites. The dish is made with standard fish chowder ingredients, but the presentation is different. It is eaten on a plate, not in a chowder bowl.

- 1 striper, about 3 pounds
- 4 slices salt pork (or bacon)
- 2 medium onions, diced
- 3 or 4 medium "Irish" potatoes, diced
- 1 tablespoon "Wooster" sauce
- salt and black pepper to taste

Dice the salt pork or bacon and sauté in a stove-top Dutch oven until the cracklings are browed and crisp. Drain the cracklings and save. Add the onions and cook until they start to brown around the edges. Add the potatoes, barely cover with water, bring to a light boil, and cook until the potatoes are tender. Add the fish, salt, pepper, and a little Wooster sauce to taste. Simmer for 15 minutes—but do not stir. Spoon servings of the muddle onto individual plates, retaining the layers as much as possible. Sprinkle each serving with a few cracklings. Enjoy.

Filipino Fish Steaks

The next time you catch a rather large striper, have your butcher cut it into steaks about 1 inch thick. A fillet will also work—but steaking the fish gives a different texture.

- 4 striper steaks
- juice and zest of 1 lime
- 1 cup olive oil
- 1 large onion, minced
- 10 cloves of garlic, crushed
- 1 tomato, diced
- 2 tablespoons fish sauce

Sprinkle the steaks with lime juice and marinate for about 30 minutes. Heat about half of the olive oil in a skillet and sauté for 5 minutes on each side. Drain the steaks. Add the rest of the oil to the skillet. Stir-fry the onions and garlic for a few minutes. Stir in the tomatoes, cooking a few more minutes. Stir in the fish sauce and a little water. Simmer until thickened to a sauce. Serve the fish steaks on a bed of rice, spooning the skillet sauce over all.

Striper Stew

Here's a stew to feed a dozen folks, or more. It can be made from one rather large striper, 15 pounds or so, or several smaller ones. The recipe also works for 3 or 4 hybrids. One of the large outdoor turkey fryers works nicely for this, rigged with a tall pot.

- 15 pounds striper or hybrid bass (dressed weight)
- 6 pounds red potatoes, quartered
- 6 pounds fresh or canned tomatoes, chopped
- 6 pounds onions, chopped
- 1 can tomato paste (4-ounce size)
- ½ pound butter
- ½ pound bacon
- Worcestershire sauce
- Tabasco sauce
- salt and pepper to taste

Put the fish in a tall stockpot. Cover with water, bring to heat, and simmer (do not boil) for half an hour. Remove the fish. Put the potatoes in the broth and cook for 20 minutes. Meanwhile, flake all the meat off the striped bass and set aside, discarding the bones.

To the pot add the tomatoes and tomato paste. Cook for 10 minutes, then add the flaked fish. Cook the bacon in a large skillet until crisp. Put the bacon drippings and the bacon (crumbled) into the pot with the fish. Season to taste with salt, pepper, Worcestershire sauce, and Tabasco sauce. Simmer for an hour or longer, stirring frequently to discourage sticking and burning. Serve hot in bowls, with plenty of chewy French bread for sopping. Leftovers should be frozen in small plastic containers.

Poached Striper with Avocado Mayonnaise

Striped bass poach nicely, and can be served hot or cold. This one is best when served cold for lunch on a warm day. Although fillets are specified, whole fish can also be used if cooked a little longer. Good store-bought mayonnaise made with real lemon juice can be used, or you can make your own using the recipe in chapter 16.

- 2 pounds boneless striper fillets
- 3 cups court bouillon (recipe in chapter 16)
- 1 very ripe avocado
- 1 cup mayonnaise
- juice and zest of 1 large lime
- fine sea salt and white pepper

Heat the court bouillon and poach the fish fillets for about 10 minutes, until they flake easily when tested with a fork. (The ideal cooking time will depend on the thickness of the fish. Allow 10 minutes per inch of thickness.) Carefully drain and remove the fish to a serving platter and refrigerate for an hour or longer.

When you are ready to serve, mash the avocado in a small bowl with a fork. Mix in the mayonnaise, lime juice (holding the zest back), sea salt, and white pepper to taste. Carefully place fillets onto a serving platter or plate. Slather each fillet with some of the avocado mayonnaise and sprinkle lightly with lime zest.

For a light lunch, you may want to serve a fillet on a bed of lettuce or a large lettuce leaf.

Rockfish Cakes

Here's a good old Scottish recipe for the thrifty use of leftover poached striper or other leftover fish.

- 8 ounces cooked fish, flaked
- 2 tablespoons melted butter
- 8 ounces mashed potatoes
- salt and pepper to taste
- two chicken eggs
- dry bread crumbs
- oil for deep frying

Rig for deep-frying at 375 degrees. Melt the butter in a small saucepan. Mix in the fish flakes and mashed potatoes. Add salt and pepper to taste, along with one of the eggs (lightly beaten). Turn the mixture out onto a floured board. Shape into patties. Roll each in beaten egg and then in bread crumbs. Deep fry until golden brown. Remove with a strainer or slotted spoon and drain on a brown bag or paper towels. Serve hot with a meal.

Stuffed Tomatoes

Anglers like to cook a whole striper, whether or not they need all of it to fill the company. Leftovers are common. This dish hits the spot, using boiled, baked, or fried fish, flaked.

- 6 medium tomatoes
- 1 cup cooked fish flakes
- ½ cup soft bread crumbs
- dry bread crumbs
- 2 tablespoons minced onion
- 2 tablespoons bacon drippings
- melted butter
- salt and black pepper to taste

Preheat the oven to 450 degrees. Cut the end off each tomato and scoop out the seeds and pulp. Heat the bacon drippings in a saucepan. Add the soft bread crumbs, and minced onion. Cook and stir for a few minutes, then stir in the fish flakes, heating through.

Stuff the tomatoes with the filling and arrange them on a baking sheet. Sprinkle the tops lightly with dry bread crumbs and brush with melted butter. Cook in the center of the oven for 10 minutes. Serve hot on lettuce, along with bacon and toast on the side.

The General's Soufflé

In his book *A General's Diary of Treasured Recipes,* General Frank Dorn said he devised this recipe during childhood to make his catch acceptable to his family. I have cooked it several times, and I recommend it for the same purpose, using stripers or other good fish of firm white flesh. The General used all green peppers in his version, but I have seen fit to use half green bell pepper and half red bell pepper, just for a touch of color. If you want to get a little frisky with the recipe, try minced jalapeño and cherry peppers, at your own risk.

1 ½ pounds of skinless striper fillets
6 chicken eggs
½ cup finely chopped onion
¼ cup finely chopped green peppers
¼ cup finely chopped red bell peppers
1 cup cream

Preheat the oven to 400 degrees. Separate the chicken eggs. Beat the yolks. Beat the whites. Mince the fish, place it into a suitable bowl, and work it with your hand, mashing it to make a rather smooth texture. Mix in the onions, peppers, cream, and beaten egg yolks. Gently fold in the egg whites. Place the mixture into a buttered casserole suitable for serving. Cook in the center of the oven for 45 minutes. Serve hot and fluffy.

Mock Shrimp, Two Ways

At one time, stripers were being cut into fingers, steamed, and served as mock-shrimp finger food, along with a suitable dipping sauce (such as Nuoc Cham). I like them even better when fried, as the main event in a meal, along with vegetables, bread, and salad. The mock shrimp idea—either fried or steamed—also works on a buffet table or as an appetizer.

Use small stripers, or perhaps white bass, and cut the fillets crosswise into fingers. For frying, it's best to leave the skin on. When cooked, the fingers will curl, making the morsel look indeed rather like a shrimp. These can be cooked in a skillet, but a deep-fryer works best for a large batch.

small stripers or whites
fine cornmeal or flour
salt
oil for deep frying
Nuoc Cham (recipe in chapter 16)

Rig for deep-frying at 375 degrees. Salt the fish fingers, roll in cornmeal or flour, and fry, a few at a time, until golden brown. Drain well on brown bags or absorbent paper. Keep warm. Serve with Nuoc Cham dipping sauce.

Or for "boiled shrimp," try steaming the striper fingers instead of boiling them. This will produce a firmer, shrimp-like flesh. Rig a steamer and bring the water to a rapid boil. Put the shrimp fingers in a single layer in the steamer insert. Steam for 5 or 6 minutes. Drain and chill for serving.

If you've got plenty of fish, why not serve these both ways?

Salt-Mound Rockfish

Since ancient times humans have been harvesting salt from the sea and salt marshes. This recipe, or cooking technique, was developed in areas where salt was free for the taking. The salt is used as a cooking medium as well as a seasoning. I have used the method to cook venison roasts, pheasants, and whole fish. Sea salt is best, but it is very expensive for landlubbers. Poor folks, and I count myself in this plight, will be advised to used the cheapest salt available. Coarse salt works best.

Note that the fish is completely covered in a mound of salt, and any food writer who tells the reader to cook until the fish is done ought to be shot. I normally cook mine in a very hot oven for 10 minutes per inch of thickness of the fish, then let it coast for a while in the hot salt. A more foolproof method is to embed a meat thermometer in the thickest part of the fish, being careful not to touch the bone. One of the new remote reading thermometers works great. Simply cook until the thermometer reads 130 degrees, then turn off the heat and let it coast a while.

Try this technique for cooking smaller fish in au gratin dishes, preparing one dish for each partaker. I find that a 12-inch white bass in an oval 13-inch au gratin dish works great.

1 whole striper, about 4 pounds
2 quarts coarse salt
white pepper
bay leaves

Preheat the oven to 400 degrees. Choose an oblong baking dish long enough to hold the fish. (The fish should be scaled and gutted, leaving the head and tail on. If it is too long, cut off the head.) Fill the bottom of the baking dish with a ½-inch bed of salt and put down a row of bay leaves. Sprinkle the fish with white pepper and put it down on the bay leaves. Add salt around the sides and build up a mound, covering the fish almost to the top. Rig the thermometer if you are using one. Top off with salt. (If you have a problem making the mound, try wetting the salt just a little, making it stick better.)

Cook until the thermometer reads 130 degrees. Then let it coast a while. After your guests have assembled around the table, put the fish in the middle. Crack the salt with a hammer (or empty wine bottle) and peel it back, letting the aroma out. Serve with steamed asparagus and a colorful salad, with hollandaise on the side.

Note that some prissified cookbooks instruct us to remove the salt in the kitchen, before the fish is put on the table. Not me. I want the show. Suit yourself. In either case, the salt will peel off in sheets, often taking the skin with it. Serve it up as best you can, making sure that most of the salt stays on the platter.

Corfiot-Style Grilled Stripers

Although the Greek isle of Corfu is noted for bianco, a stew usually made from by-catch that is too small or too ugly for the market, the fishermen themselves often prefer a grilled sea bass or other fresh fish of some size. I love stripers cooked by their method—including the optional garlic stuffing. The rigani used in the recipe is the flower heads of oregano. It can sometimes be purchased in Greek markets. If necessary, substitute a little Greek oregano. Allow a whole fish for each person.

- stripers or hybrids, about 2 pounds each
- sea salt
- olive oil
- lemon juice
- rigani (or Greek oregano)
- whole garlic cloves, peeled

Rig for grilling over charcoal or wood coals. Scale and gut the fish. Remove the fins (being sure to cut out the bony spines), but leave on the head and tails. Lightly score the fish several times from head to tail. Sprinkle inside and out with a little sea salt. Mix some lemon juice and olive oil, along with a little rigani. Set aside until the coals are hot.

Grease the grill and position it about 6 inches over the hot coals. (If you put them too close to the coals, the outside of the fish will get done before the garlic is soft and nutty flavored.) Brush the fish inside and out with part of the lemon sauce. Stuff the cavity of each fish with whole garlic cloves. Grease the grill to help prevent sticking. Grill the fish, basting, carefully turning, and moving the fish every few minutes. Cook and turn, cook and turn, until the fish flakes easily and the head is ready to fall off. A little smoke from the coals helps, but do not baste with too much olive oil. It helps to have a large grill for this, giving you plenty of room to maneuver.

Serve hot along with plenty of good Greek bread, a hearty green salad, and a dressing made of leftover basting sauce or a new mix.

Gullah Macaroni

The narrator of one of my favorite regional Gullah cookbooks jokes that "Yankee Doodle went to town for to git macaroni. I don't know whether he went to Charleston or to Savannah, but I sho glad he git 'em." I'm glad too. Most children also like macaroni, making this a good one for those who haven't yet acquired a taste for fish.

- 1 pounds striper fillet
- 2 ounces macaroni
- 1 tablespoon melted butter, plus a little more
- 1 cup top milk or half-and-half
- 2 tablespoons flour
- 1 tablespoon fine white bread crumbs
- salt and pepper to taste

Boil the macaroni in water until tender, following the directions on the package. Drain it and cut it into ½-inch segments. Preheat the oven to 350 degrees. Cut the fish into ½-inch dice.

Mix the melted butter, milk, and flour in a bowl. Add the fish, cooked macaroni, salt, and pepper. Dump the mix into a greased pie dish, spread it out evenly, and sprinkle lightly with bread crumbs. Dribble a little melted butter on top. Cook in the center of the oven for about 30 minutes, or until the top of the pie is a light brown color. Give thanks to Yankee Doodle and enjoy.

Baked Stripers

Baking whole fish, head on, is an excellent way to show off the angler's catch, and stripers are quite attractive when cooked by this method. The fish should be scaled and gutted, leaving head, fins, and tail intact. Fish 4 or 5 pounds work best, but larger ones can be baked. As a rule, the cooking time in a 350 degree oven is 10 minutes per inch of thickness. So, modify the recipe to suit your catch.

1 striper, 4 or 5 pounds
1 stick butter (divided)
4 slices bacon
small red "new" potatoes
sea salt and freshly ground black pepper
lemon slices for garnish

Preheat the oven to 350 degrees. Grease the bottom of a baking dish or pan of suitable size with butter. Brush the fish inside and out with melted butter and sprinkle with salt and pepper. Place the fish in the baking pan and cover with strips of bacon. Bake for 40 or 50 minutes (depending on dressed weight) in the center of the oven. While waiting, peel and boil the small new potatoes in a pot until fork tender. Baste the fish from time to time with pan drippings

When the fish is almost done, drain the potatoes and place them around the fish, rolling in the pan drippings to coat all over. When the fish flakes easily when tested with a fork, carefully remove it to a serving platter. Arrange the new potatoes all around it. Spoon the pan juices over all. Serve with lemon wedges or slices, along with a chewy bread, green beans, chef's salad, or whatever you want with your baked fish. I'll take a little wine with mine, thank you. Red will be fine.

A.D.'s Pickled Chain Pickerel (p. 59)

Pike, Pickerel, and Muskellunge

Ukrainian Pike, Finnish Pike, Peloponnesian Pike, and a Southern Fried Jack for Junior Samples

Several species of pike-like fish are available to North American anglers. The northern pike, sometimes called the great northern pike, is perhaps the most important of these. It grows naturally from New York to Nebraska, and has been introduced in other areas. It also grows in Northern Europe and around to Siberia, making it a truly circumpolar species. No freshwater fish has been more important in myth and story than the pike—the water wolf.

The walleye is often called "walleyed pike," but they are an unrelated fish and were covered in the previous chapter. Several species of pickerel grow in North America. The largest of these, the chain pickerel, grows from Canada to Florida, where they are often taken by bass anglers. The chain pickerel grows to 9 pounds or so, although the average is 2 or 3 pounds. The smaller pickerel species include the grass pickerel and the redfin pickerel (both called littler pickerel, with a maximum length of 10 or 12 inches). All of the pickerels are good eating, if properly prepared, and look pretty much alike.

The heavyweight of the pike family is the muskellunge, or muskie, weighing up to 50 or 60 pounds. There are several subspecies. The muskie is mostly a fish of the Northeast and Great Lakes, south to the Tennessee River system. The muskie is good eating, but these days the really large ones are usually released—or put on the wall with the elk mounts.

Isaac Walton of *The Compleat Angler* immortality wrote about a pike roasted on a spit, somehow trussed with sticks of birch or other sweet wood. The recipe called for a stuffing made from butter, anchovy fillets, pickled oysters, and shredded pike liver. It was basted with a mix of claret wine, crushed anchovies, and butter. Since I can't figure out exactly how Walton spitted the pike (unscaled, we are told), I have not tried to reconstruct the how-to part of the recipe. Jackleg camp chefs can have fun with this, though. So, have at it.

Many are the European recipes for pike. The Bavarians of old, for example, loved a dish called Pike Hechtenkraut, cooked with onions, bread crumbs, and sauerkraut. Some of the pike recipes below reflect this European heritage. I find it interesting, however, that the pike was not a favorite of the American Indians and, in general, is not highly rated as table fare in American even today. So . . . go figure.

In any case, all of the pike family have small bones embedded in the flesh, a problem often ignored in European recipes. In general, the bigger the fish, the easier it is to remove the bones either before cooking or at the table. The pickerels, being smaller, are especially bony. There are also ways to nullify the bones, as explained in some of the recipes. (See especially A.D.'s Pickled Chain Pickerel, Gefilte Fish, and Fried Jack for Junior Samples.) In general, all these fish have relatively dry flesh and should not be cooked too long by direct-heat methods.

Try these suggestions.

Pike with Anchovy

Here's an interesting dish of Austrian tradition, adapted here from *Austrian Cooking and Baking*.

- I pike short enough to fit a large baking pan
- butter
- canned anchovy fillets
- butter
- more butter

Scale and draw the pike. Make shallow crosswise slits on either side, spaced about an inch apart. Preheat the oven to 375 degrees. Melt a little butter in the pan. Cut the anchovy fillets into thin slivers and stuff these in the slits. Put the pike into the baking pan and roll to coat both sides with butter. Bake for about 30 minutes (basting a time or two with melted butter from the pan) until the pike flakes easily when tested with a fork.

While waiting, pound several anchovy fillets into a paste with mortar and pestle. Melt ¼ cup of butter in a pan and stir in the anchovy. Put the pike onto a heated serving platter and pour the anchovy sauce over it. Serve hot with new potatoes, steamed carrots, green salad, and bread.

Ukrainian Pike with Dried Mushrooms

The Ukrainians have an unusual method of cooking pike, walleye, and other good fish, adapted here from *The Best of Ukrainian Cuisine*. The dried mushrooms really make the dish. I dry my own chanterelles, but any good dried mushroom will do.

- 2 pounds fresh pike, cut into 2-inch chunks
- I cup dried mushrooms
- 2 medium onions
- oil
- 2 pounds new potatoes
- 3 or 4 bay leaves
- I cup dry bread crumbs
- salt and black pepper to taste

Soak the mushrooms in water in a pot for 30 minutes. Add some salt, bring to heat, and simmer for 30 minutes. While waiting, sauté the onions in a little oil. Drain and set aside.

Drain and chop the mushrooms, being sure to save the water in which they were cooked. Slice the new potatoes and simmer them in a separate pot until tender. Drain and set aside.

Put the fish chunks, mushrooms, sautéed onions, and potatoes into a pot. Add the bay leaves, salt, pepper, and 1 cup of the reserved mushroom water. Mix gently and simmer for 20 minutes.

While waiting, preheat the oven to 325 degrees. Using a slotted spoon, take the fish chunks out of the mixture, roll in bread crumbs, put into a greased pan, and bake for 10 minutes. Plate the fish, putting the potatoes and mushrooms all around.

Gypsy Fish Cakes

A lot of old recipes call for mixing mashed potatoes into flaked leftover fish. Fried, poached, baked, grilled—whatever you've got. Of course, freshly cooked fish can also be used.

- ½ pound cooked fish flakes
- 2 medium to large potatoes
- 2 chicken eggs (lightly whisked separately)
- 1 cup dry bread crumbs
- 1 tablespoon butter
- 1 tablespoon chopped fresh parsley
- lard (or cooking oil) for frying
- salt and black pepper

Boil the potatoes until tender, then mash them until all the lumps are gone. Using your hands, mix in the fish flakes, parsley, salt, and pepper, along with a lightly whisked egg. Shape the mixture into a log on a cutting board and cut into 8 slices. (If the cutting disfigures the slices, shape them with your hands into round patties.)

Roll-coat patties with whisked egg and roll in bread crumbs. Set aside while you heat some lard or oil, getting it almost hot enough to spit back at you. Fry the fish patties until golden and crisp on both sides. Drain and serve hot. Feeds two to four.

Pike Loaf

This is a good recipe to try when you or your family are tired of eating pike or pickerel. It's best to poach some fresh fish, but leftovers from fried or baked fish can also be used.

- 3 cups precooked pike flakes
- 2 cups bread crumbs
- 2 large chicken eggs, whisked
- 2 tablespoons butter
- 1 teaspoon Worcestershire sauce
- juice and grated zest of ½ lemon
- salt and black pepper to taste
- ketchup or tomato-based salsa

Preheat the oven to 350 degrees and grease a loaf pan. With your hands, mix all the ingredients except the ketchup or salsa in a bowl. Also using your hands, press the mixture into the pan. Bake in the center of the oven for 45 minutes.

Brush the top of the loaf heavily with ketchup or smear on some salsa. Return to the oven and cook for another 15 minutes. Serve hot or warm. Or chill and slice for sandwiches, slathering the bread with hollandaise sauce or a good mayonnaise (recipes in chapter 16).

Pike with Sour Cream

Here's an unusual cooking technique that works with sour cream stuffing. Be sure to try it.

- 4-pound northern pike, scaled and gutted
- 3 cups bread crumbs
- 1 cup chopped celery with green tops
- 1 cup chopped onion
- ¾ cup sour cream
- ¼ cup melted butter
- juice and grated zest of 1 lime
- 1 teaspoon minced fresh thyme
- salt and pepper to taste

Preheat the oven to 350 degrees and grease a baking pan long enough to hold the pike. Salt and pepper the pike inside and out, then bake in the center of the oven for 30 minutes. While waiting, sauté the onions and celery in butter until tender. Stir in the sour cream, lime juice, zest, bread crumbs, salt, pepper, and thyme.

After 30 minutes, remove the pike from the oven and carefully fill it with the sour cream stuffing. Return to the oven and bake for another 10 minutes. Enjoy with rice, vegetables or salad, and bread.

Finnish Stuffed Pike

The Finns use an unusual stuffing for baked pike. Be sure to try it with a small northern. I have adapted the recipe from Alan Davidson's *North Atlantic Seafood*.

- 3-pound pike
- 1 cup cooked rice
- 2 hard-boiled eggs, chopped
- 8 to 10 chopped prunes
- 3 tablespoons heavy cream plus a little more
- melted butter
- toasted bread crumbs
- salt and freshly ground black pepper

Scale and gut the pike, sprinkle it inside and out with salt, and set aside for an hour or so. Preheat the oven to 375 degrees. Stuff the fish with a mixture of the rice, eggs, prunes, cream, salt and pepper. Brush the fish with melted butter and dredge in bread crumbs. In a greased pan, bake it in the center of the oven for 45 minutes, basting from time to time with a mixture of water and cream. The fish is done when the fins pull off easily. Serve hot.

Poor Man's Lobster

Here's a good one from Dan Gapen, son of Don Gapen, inventor of the Muddler Minnow. Dan used pike fillets, but other fish with firm flesh, such as stripers or whitefish, will do.

4 pounds northern pike fillets
2 sticks butter, melted
3 ribs celery, chopped
1 large onion, chopped
1 cup dry white wine
½ cup freshly squeezed lemon juice
3 quarts water
paprika
salt to taste

Heat the water in a pot. Add wine, lemon juice, celery, onion, and salt. While the pot simmers for a few minutes, cut the pike fillets into 2-inch chunks and preheat the broiler.

Put the fish into the pot, bring to a new boil, reduce the heat, and simmer for 5 or 6 minutes. Drain the fish, dry, and place on a broiling pan. Brush with melted butter. Broil for 5 minutes. Turn the fish, brush with melted butter, and broil for 2 or 3 minutes. Sprinkle with paprika and serve as finger food. A lemon butter dipping sauce (recipe in chapter 16) hits the spot.

A.D.'s Pickled Chain Pickerel

I may have pickled a world's record chain pickerel, caught in Lake Weir, Florida, where I used to live on Timucuan Island. Had my writing office in the boathouse, but spent too much time fishing. How big was the fish? As long as a boat paddle, it seemed. Unfortunately, I neglected to weigh or measure the thing, but it made more than a gallon of pickles.

In any case, the pickling process dissolves or softens the small bones in pickerel, suckers, carp, and other fish that have tiny bones embedded in the fillet.

I always skin the fillets and cut them into fingers and cut them crosswise into strips from about ½ to ¾ inch wide and about 2 inches long. These bite-sized pickles are easy to handle, and sit nicely atop a cracker. The measurements in the recipe can be increased if you want lots of pickles and have a world-class fish, or several smaller ones.

It's best to put them up in wide-mouth quart jars. The pickling spices can be purchased at spice sections of most supermarkets, or you can mix your own, including bay leaves, allspice berries, peppercorns, cloves, etc. I prefer to use the commercial or Louisiana crab boil spices, packaged in convenient little cloth bags.

1 pound pickerel fingers
1 cup sea salt
1 bag crab boil spices
onion, thinly sliced
red bell pepper, thinly sliced (optional)
white vinegar
water

Put 2 quarts of water into a nonmetallic container and dissolve the salt in it. (A Crock-Pot works nicely for this process.) Put the pickerel fingers into the brine and weight down with a plate or saucer or block of wood so that the brine completely covers the fish. Leave in the brine for 2 full days in a cool place.

Sterilize a wide-mouth mason jar (1 jar for each pound of fish fillet). Place the spice bag (or 2 tablespoons mixed pickling spices) in the jar. Add a layer of onion slices. (Along with each layer of onions, I like to include a thin slice of red bell pepper, just for color.) Add a layer of pickerel fingers, another slice of onion, etc., until the jar is almost full, ending with onions. Fill the jar with a mixture of half vinegar and half spring water (unchlorinated). Tap the jar all around to dislodge any air bubbles. Screw on the lid and leave in the refrigerator for 3 or 4 weeks.

These pickles will keep for a couple of months. Enjoy them as a snack atop saltines. These go nicely with beer. The pickles can also be used in salads.

Fried Jack for Junior Samples

Redneck comedian Junior Samples of *Hee Haw* fame was an avid bass angler and indeed competed in some of the big national tournaments. At such an event on Lake Seminole in Georgia, he brought several keeper bass and a 2-foot chain pickerel to the weigh-in. The tournament director laughed and said that "jacks," as chain pickerel are called in that neck of the woods, were not allowed. Of course, Junior already knew this, but he said, "Well, shoot, a jack is shore better than a bass."

Well, I know several other people who feel the same way, and they usually fry them. Most people "gash" them in one way or another to beat the bones. Here's my way. (Note: Most suckers can also be cooked by this method and may be even better.)

Scale the jack, leaving the skin attached. Fillet it and discard the backbone. Partly freeze the fillets. Take them out of the freezer, one at a time, and lay flat on a cutting board, skin-side down. Using a sharp knife, make cuts crosswise, going through the meat and down to—but not through—the skin. The cuts should be about ⅛ inch thick. Thus, the whole fillet will resemble a slab of rind-on sliced bacon. Salt and pepper the fillet, dust it in cornmeal, and fry in very hot fat (375 degrees) until browned and quite crispy. Then eat it bones and all, along with whatever you want with fried fish.

Fried Pike Backstrap

A long strip of boneless meat can be cut off the top of a pike. This strip, which resembles a pork tenderloin in shape, is delicious when cut into pieces and deep-fried.

- 2-inch pieces of pike backstrap
- flour
- yellow cornmeal
- 2 chicken eggs, lightly whisked
- salt and pepper to taste
- oil for deep frying

Heat the oil to 375 degrees. Dredge the pike pieces in flour, roll in egg, and dredge in cornmeal. Deep-fry a few pieces at a time until they float. Cook a while longer to brown nicely, paying due attention to each piece. Drain on a brown bag and serve hot, along with go-withs of your choice and hard cider.

Planked Muskellunge

Many of us like to show off a trophy catch not on the wall but on the dinner table. Short, thick fish, like a largemouth bass, are relatively easy to handle by baking or poaching in modern kitchen utensils. But a big, long muskie is another matter. If you insist on cooking the whole fish in the kitchen, I can't help you.

The best bet is to fillet the fish, skin on. Build a good fire in the fireplace and build up some coals. Nail the fillets, skin-side down, onto two hardwood planks, such as hickory or ash. Mix a baste of melted butter, sea salt, and a little white wine Worcestershire sauce. Prop the planks against the mantel with the fillets at an angle to the fire. Roast for 15 minutes, then find your heat-proof gloves and invert the planks upside-down and roast for another 15 minutes. Test for doneness. Serve the fish on the planks.

For more on plank cookery, both pro and con, see the Planked Salmon in chapter 3.

Peloponnesian Pike Fillets

Here's a Greek recipe that works with northern pike, muskie, or large pickerel. If you are on a budget, use peanut oil instead of olive oil for frying. If you are on a really tight budget, use the cheapest vegetable oil in the supermarket.

2 pounds pike fillets
juice and zest of 2 lemons
1 ½ cups sour cream
1 cup olive or peanut oil for skillet-frying
flour
salt and black pepper to taste
1 teaspoon fresh Greek oregano, minced

Put the fillets into a bowl. Add the lemon juice, zest, salt, and pepper, tossing to coat all sides of the fish. Refrigerate for several hours. When you are ready to cook, heat the oil in a skillet to 375 degrees. While the oil heats, put some flour, salt, and black pepper into a bag. Shake the fillets and set aside. Fry the fillets a few pieces at a time until golden brown on both sides. Set aside to drain on a brown bag. Pour off most of the oil, retaining about ¼ cup of it and all the little brown bits from the bottom. Brown the oregano. Add the left-over marinade and sour cream. Cook and stir with a wooden spoon until you have a nice sauce. Arrange the fish on a serving platter and pour the sauce over all. Serve hot, along with a huge Greek salad and some good chewy Greek bread.

Gefilte Fish

This old Jewish dish was originally made by first skinning a fish and then stuffing the skin with a mixture of ground fish, chicken eggs, matzo meal, and other ingredients. After being stuffed, the fish was poached, cut into slices, and simmered in a broth. In time the stuffed skin idea was abandoned, partly because of the difficulty of skinning intact (easy only with eels). The skin is usually omitted entirely these days, but it's best to use it in making the broth, if you like.

The success of the dish, some say, is in grinding the flesh into a paste. To accomplish this, I zap it in a food processor or blender, then smooth it down with a mortar and pestle. Then "chop" the mixture vigorously. (Chopping is best done in a wooden bowl with a hand-held chopper with contoured blade.) The purpose of all this is to work air into the ground fish mixture—which is the secret to the quintessential gefilte fish. This takes patience, time, tender loving care, and a strong arm. Anyone in too much of a hurry to shoot for perfection can simply zap the fish mixture longer.

Traditionally, the dish is made with more than one kind of fish, and often includes carp and pike. I am using the smaller chain pickerel here simply because the bones in this fish are something of a problem as compared to the larger pike. The zapping and the pounding will render the bones harmless, if you do a good job. When you fillet the fish, be sure to save the skin.

½ pound pickerel fillets
½ pound carp fillets
½ pound drum or other white-fleshed fish
fish heads, bones, and skin
2 medium carrots, diced
2 medium onions, diced
2 chicken eggs
2 tablespoons matzo meal
salt and pepper
horseradish sauce (go-with)
kosher pickles (go-with)
grated raw carrots (go-with)
lemon wedges (go with)
salt and pepper to taste
water
ice water

Add 3 pints water to a saucepan and bring to heat. Add half the carrots and onions, along with the fish heads, bones, and skin. Cover and simmer for an hour or longer, then strain out and discard the vegetables and fish parts. (Well, save the heads for picking and nibbling in private.)

While waiting for the broth to mature, finely grind the fish as described above along with the rest of the carrots and onions. In a large bowl, combine the fish mixture, eggs, matzo meal, 2 tablespoons of ice water, salt, and pepper. Beat vigorously with a whisk (using even more elbow grease) until the mixture is rather fluffy. Use your hands to shape the mixture into balls a little larger than a golf ball but smaller than a tennis ball. Or make ovals.

Place the balls into the broth and simmer for 20 minutes. Remove carefully and drain on brown bags. Serve either hot or cold, along with horseradish, pickles, grated carrots, and lemon wedges. This is great everyday noshing fare as well as traditional Jewish food for the Sabbath or holidays.

Note also that the balls can be flattened, dredged in matzo meal, and fried in a skillet. Loaf slices can also be dredged and fried. Good stuff.

Whitefish

Whitefish with Pomegranate Sauce, Whitefish Burgers, Whitefish Kabobs, and Other Enticing Recipes for an Unsung Gamefish, with a Nod to the Cisco

Why so many trout anglers cuss whenever they catch a whitefish has always been a mystery to me. These fish readily take artificial flies, put up a good fight, make excellent table fare, and should be targeted by any fly-rodder who likes to eat fish but feels guilty about keeping a trout or two. I don't expect to change many minds with a few words here—but perhaps giving the unsung whitefish whole-chapter status will get some attention.

And why not? The whitefish are one of the most popular market fish in the world. They are especially good when smoked.

There are several species in North America. The lake whitefish is common in Maine and some other Northern states, as well as in Canada. The average catch is 3 or 4 pounds, but this species grows up to 20 pounds. As the name implies, they are usually found in lakes, but they also enter rivers during spring and fall.

The mountain whitefish is found mostly in lakes and streams on the western slopes of the Rocky Mountains from Northern California to British Columbia. It feeds extensively on flies and nymphs, and is often taken by anglers after trout. Mountain whitefish grow up to 5 pounds, but they usually average about 2 pounds. They are excellent when fried, and make a good shore lunch for those anglers who release all their trout.

Round whitefish are widely distributed across North America, Canada, and Alaska, on into Siberia. This species is much smaller than the lake whitefish, and it is not as good on the table. It does not keep well. Eat it fresh, or salted, not smoked.

Some eight species of cisco live in North American waters, mostly in the large lakes from New England to the Great Lakes and North into Canada. Closely related to whitefish, they are excellent game fish and table fish, but are seldom caught by most anglers owing to their deep-water habits. In winter, they are taken through the ice. In summer, however, they will rise for the mayfly hatch and can be taken on the fly. The cisco is very good when smoked, and can be used in recipes for whitefish. The cisco grows all around the Arctic and is popular table fare in Finland, Sweden, and elsewhere.

Here are a few recipes to try for whichever kind of whitefish you are lucky enough to catch.

Wilza Robertson's Whitefish Chowder (p. 66)

Hot-Smoked Whitefish

Every jackleg patio cook in the country will have a recipe and method of hot-smoking fish, and most will be ready to argue the merits of hickory over mesquite, or vice versa. Their method often depends on what kind of grill or cooker they are using. Here's one for the popular silo-shaped units with a water pan. The recipe can be adapted for large covered grills and the double-barrel rigs.

- 3 pounds whitefish fillets
- 2 quarts water
- ¾ cup salt
- ½ cup dark brown sugar
- 1 teaspoon black pepper
- bacon drippings
- 2 bay leaves
- hardwood chips

Mix the water, salt, brown sugar, and pepper. Pour the mixture over the fillets in a nonmetallic container. Refrigerate overnight, stirring the mixture a time or two.

The next day, drain the fish and heat the silo (gas or charcoal) cooker. Fill the water pan with water and add the bay leaves. Fill the smoke pan with wood chips. Brush the fillets with bacon drippings and place on the racks. Close the lid. Cook and smoke until the fish are golden brown on top and flake easily when tested with a fork. Thanks to the water pan, the fish will be moist and succulent—but do not overcook.

Cold Smoked Whitefish

I start hemming and hawing every time I have to write something on this subject. To be safe for human consumption, much depends on having a good salt cure, and, these days, many health food freaks preach that salt is poison. Fact is, salt is a natural preservative and inhibits the growth of bacteria. Omit it in cold-smoked fish (and jerky) at your peril, both culinary and otherwise.

Instead of bogging down a lengthy cold smoking recipe here, I have decided to add this material in Appendix II. It can, of course, be used with whitefish and some other species available to the angler.

Smoked Fish & Egg Scramble

I enjoy this dish with any leftover fish. It is especially good with leftover hot-smoked whitefish.

- 1 cup hot-smoked whitefish, flaked
- 4 large chicken eggs
- 2 to 4 scallions, chopped with part of green tops
- 2 tablespoons butter
- salt and freshly ground black pepper to taste

Whisk the eggs and mix in the whitefish flakes and scallions. Heat the butter in a cast iron skillet. Cook on medium heat, scrambling as you go, until the eggs are set. Sprinkle with salt and pepper to taste. Serve hot. This makes a hearty breakfast for two or three, or a light lunch served with buttered toast and sliced red-ripe tomatoes.

Gilroy Whitefish

This one probably won't win any prizes at the annual Garlic Festival in Gilroy, California, because it is too simple. But it sure is good, and it makes a good camp or shore lunch fry because you don't have to tote along a lot of stuff. It's also a good one for the kitchen if you are cooking for anyone who doesn't like the way a fish smells.

Rocky Mountain whitefish fillets
garlic salt
whole garlic cloves
cooking oil

Sprinkle the fillets on both sides with garlic salt. Heat a little oil in a skillet on medium-high heat and fry the garlic cloves whole. (There is no need to peel the garlic, as the husk is easy to remove after frying and sometimes comes off in the skillet.) Fry until the inside of the garlic turns nicely brown and the husks start coming off in the skillet. Remove the garlic and drain it on a brown bag.

Sauté the fish on medium-high heat until they are browned nicely on both sides. Serve with the fried garlic, plenty of lightly toasted garlic bread, and a colorful salad with a garlicky dressing. All joking aside, fried garlic is a very good accompaniment to fried fish.

Wilza Robertson's Whitefish Chowder

Most old-time chowder recipes called for hardtack, but modern variations scale down to chowder crackers or oyster crackers, or biscuits. The chowder here is adapted from *The Maine Way,* a collection of unprissified fish and game recipes, published by the Maine Department of Inland Fisheries and Wildlife. Oh, it's so good—and so sensible. Wilza says to nail the fish by the head to a tree or post to aid in skinning it. Note also that smoked whitefish make a purely excellent chowder.

whitefish, "skint" and cut into pieces to fit the pot
6 large Maine potatoes, diced
1 large onion, diced
fried bacon
2 quarts whole milk
salted water
biscuits, cooked separately

Put the fish in a suitable pot, cover with salted water, and simmer for 30 minutes. Remove the fish pieces, debone, and add the flesh back to the pot. Add the diced potatoes, onion, and several slices of bacon, crumbled. Simmer until the potato is done, and very little liquid remains in the pot. Add the milk. Bring to heat, but do not boil. Serve in bowls with plenty of hot biscuits. I'll take a twist or two of that freshly ground black pepper on mine. Hunker down for seconds.

Smoked Fish on a Shingle

This dish can be made with leftover fish, and it is especially good with smoked whitefish.

- 2 cups fish flakes
- 1 cup bacon drippings or cooking oil
- 1 cup flour
- 1 cup fish stock (recipe in chapter 16)
- 1 cup milk
- salt and black pepper to taste
- toast

Heat the oil and flour in a deep skillet, stirring until you have a light roux. Add the fish stock, milk, fish flakes, salt, and pepper. Cook for a few minutes, stirring constantly. Serve hot over toast, adding a little more freshly ground black pepper if wanted.

Whitefish Steaks Provençale

Cut the whitefish into steaks about ¾ inch thick. Fillets can also be used, but these should not be called steaks.

- 3 or 4 pounds whitefish steaks
- ¼ cup olive oil (more if needed)
- 1 cup chopped onion
- 10 cloves garlic, peeled
- 4 medium tomatoes, chopped
- 1 tablespoon minced parsley
- 1 teaspoon tarragon leaves
- ½ cup chablis
- sea salt and black pepper to taste

Salt and pepper the steaks lightly and sauté 3 or 4 at a time in olive oil. Set aside to drain. Keep warm. Add a little more olive oil as you go, as needed.

When all the steaks have been cooked, sauté the onions and garlic until soft. Add the tomatoes, parsley, tarragon, chablis, salt, and pepper. Increase the heat and simmer until you have a chunky sauce. Serve the steaks on individual plates, topping each with 2 tablespoons of the sauce. Serve with French bread and more chablis, along with steamed asparagus, salad, or whatever you want with your fish steaks.

Whitefish with Pomegranate and Walnut Sauce

Here's a cold fish dish from the Republic of Georgia, where both pomegranates and walnuts are important culinary ingredients.

- 4 whitefish fillets (about 2 pounds total)
- 2 tablespoons flour
- ½ cup English walnut pieces
- 2 large garlic cloves, peeled
- 1 tablespoon hot pepper, seeded and minced
- ½ cup pomegranate juice
- 2 tablespoons tomato paste
- oil for frying (about half a cup)
- 1 tablespoon butter
- 2 medium onions, chopped
- sea salt and freshly ground black pepper
- pomegranate seeds for garnish
- water

Sprinkle the fish with salt and pepper. Shake in a bag with the flour. Dust off the excess flour and set aside while you make the sauce. Grind the walnuts and garlic, adding about ½ teaspoon sea salt. Stir in the minced hot pepper, ½ cup water, pomegranate juice, and tomato paste. Mix well and set aside to let the flavors blend.

Heat about ½ inch of oil in a skillet. Fry the fish for about 8 minutes, turn, and fry for another 8 minutes, or until golden brown and crispy outside. Drain and place in a shallow heat-proof casserole dish suitable for serving.

In another skillet, sauté the onion in the butter for 8 minutes or so. Spread the onions over the fish. Pour the sauce over all, bring to a quick boil, reduce the heat, and simmer, covered, for 2 minutes. Remove the casserole dish from the heat and let the fish cool. Refrigerate until needed. Serve chilled. This makes a nice lunch on a hot day, garnished with a few fresh pomegranate seeds, if available.

Whitefish Burgers

These burgers can be eaten like fish cakes, or used in a hamburger bun. Those who like hash browns for breakfast will also love this dish. Use either leftover fish, or steam and flake some whitefish fillets. These patties are especially good with leftover hot-smoked whitefish.

- 2 cups flaked whitefish (precooked)
- 2 medium potatoes, grated
- 1 medium onion, minced
- 2 chicken eggs, whisked
- salt and pepper to taste
- butter for frying

Mix the fish flakes, grated potatoes, minced onion, eggs, salt, and pepper. Shape into patties and set aside to set for a few minutes. Heat some butter in a skillet. On medium heat, sauté the patties 1 or 2 at the time for 4 or 5 minutes on each side. (Make sure that the grated potatoes are done. If in doubt, you may want to cook the potatoes in the skillet before mixing with the fish.)

Serve as a pattie or in a hamburger bun. In either case, a topping of hollandaise sauce (see recipe in chapter 16) will hit the spot. If making a burger, a single slice from a very large tomato works nicely.

The General's Choice

Brigadier General Frank Dorn, gourmet and raconteur, loved whitefish livers, which he said were better for this recipe than those from chicken or duck. If you don't have enough whitefish livers to cook the dish, add a few chicken livers from the supermarket. I might add that some other fish livers, and turtle livers, are very good, but my editor advises me not to push this too far.

- 6 to 10 whitefish livers
- ½ cup brandy
- ½ cup dry white wine
- ½ cup butter
- 8 peppercorns
- 8 whole cloves
- 4 bay leaves
- 2 tablespoons Worcestershire sauce
- 1 teaspoon ground ginger
- 1 teaspoon caraway seeds
- 2 shakes Tabasco sauce
- sea salt and freshly ground black pepper

Set the livers aside. Put all the other ingredients in a saucepan, bring to a boil, and simmer for 2 or 3 minutes to mingle the flavors. Add the livers and place in the refrigerator for 6 hours or longer.

When you are ready to proceed, preheat the broiler. Drain the livers (saving the sauce) and broil until golden brown on both sides. Strain the sauce into a pan. Add a little flour and cook, stirring as you go, until the sauce thickens a little. Arrange the livers on a serving platter and pour the sauce over them.

Serve hot, garnished, the General says, with white radishes.

Whitefish Roe

If the General's choice suggestion above doesn't whet your appetite, at least try the roe The eggs are quite small as compared to trout eggs (which can become a little too rubbery for comfort). The white roe is also very good and can be cooked like mullet white roe (see chapter 15). I like to dust these with flour, but extra-fine cornmeal or other dusting can also be used.

- whitefish roe
- all purpose flour
- bacon and bacon drippings
- sliced mushrooms
- sea salt and black pepper to taste
- toast halves, buttered

Salt and pepper the roe sacs. Shake in a bag with flour. Dust off the excess and set aside for half an hour or so. Cook the bacon in a cast-iron skillet until crisp. Set aside to drain.

Add more bacon drippings to the skillet if needed to make up a depth of ¼ inch or better. Sauté the mushrooms for a few minutes, turning once, until tender. Remove to drain. Fry the roe on medium heat, turning a time or two, until lightly browned all around. Drain the roe on paper towels. Serve roe, mushrooms, and bacon on toast halves.

Whitefish Salad

Oddly, this recipe came to me from Wolfie Cohen's Rascal House in Miami Beach, via *Roadfood Sandwiches* by Jane and Michael Stern. This is a long way from whitefish water, but, on the other hand, smoked whitefish are popular market fare.

- 2 pounds smoked whitefish
- 2 ribs celery, diced
- 1 medium red onion, diced
- 1 cup sour cream
- 2 tablespoons mayonnaise
- 1 tablespoon minced fresh dill
- juice of ½ lemon

Remove any skin and bones from the whitefish and cut into 1-inch chunks. Using your hands, gently mix all the ingredients in a large bowl. Serve on lettuce leaves for a light lunch—or, I say, use it as a stuffing for large Florida avocados. Serve with crackers, wheat thins, or good rye bread.

The Sterns recommend using the salad as a sandwich filling. Suit yourself.

Stuffed Whitefish

Here's an easy recipe that works well with a whitefish. If your fish bears roe, add some of the egglets to the stuffing. Since the fish has a small head, squeamish folk might not find it quite as off-putting as a stuffed largemouth bass of similar size, which can also be cooked with the same recipe.

- 1 whitefish, 3 or 4 pounds
- thin strips salt pork (rind removed)
- 3 or 4 cups Cornbread Stuffing (recipe in chapter 16)
- bacon drippings or melted butter (optional)
- salt and pepper to taste

Scale and draw the fish. Sprinkle inside and out with a little salt and pepper. Set aside while you preheat the oven to 350 degrees.

Fill the fish loosely with the stuffing and close with skewers or sew with string. Place the stuffed fish in a well-greased baking pan. Top with strips of salt pork, or brush heavily with melted butter or bacon drippings. Bake in the center of the oven for 40 minutes, or until the fish flakes easily when tested with a fork. (If you aren't using the salt pork topping, it's best to baste the fish every 10 minutes or so with butter or bacon drippings.)

Place the fish on a long serving platter and remove the skewers or string. Serve hot with new potatoes, french-cut green beans, and a good bread.

Russian Whitefish Kabobs with Caviar

The Russians like to think they invented the kabob, or shashlik, but the Turks and Mongols hold different views. In any case, this Russian recipe can be cooked over gas or electric heat—but charcoal or wood is better. It's also better to cook the kabobs directly over the heat instead of putting them on a rack, if possible. Try putting two narrow concrete blocks on the ground, spaced 8 or 10 inches apart with the fire in between so that ends of the skewers can rest on either block, exposing the fish directly to the heat. This makes them easy to turn and eliminates the sticking problem.

1 pound whitefish fillets
1 pound medium button mushrooms
½ pint sour cream
¼ pound red caviar
juice of 1 lemon
dry bread crumbs
melted butter
salt and pepper to taste
small new potatoes (cooked separately)
fresh parsley, finely chopped (garnish)

Cut the fillets into kabob-size chunks. Roll them in melted butter, sprinkle with salt and pepper, and roll in the bread crumbs. Thread the fish onto skewers, alternating with mushroom caps. (You should have some mushrooms left.) Set aside and rig for grilling about 6 inches over the heat source.

Sprinkle each kabob lightly with lemon juice. Grill for 10 minutes, carefully turning a time or two. As the kabobs cook, sauté the rest of the mushrooms in butter. Set aside. In a small bowl, mix the red caviar and sour cream. Serve the kabobs hot, flanked with the mushrooms and new potatoes, garnished with the sour cream and caviar mixture. A few sprigs of parsley sprinkled on the new potatoes won't hurt a thing.

Camp Dutch Oven Whitefish

Here's a culinary treat adapted from *The Maine Way*, to which it was submitted by one Joel Fawcett of Grand Lake Stream.

1 whitefish
1 quart milk
2 cups coarse bread crumbs (cornbread will do)
½ cup minced celery
¼ cup dry white wine
1 teaspoon salt
½ teaspoon dried tarragon
¼ teaspoon black pepper

Build a good wood fire and burn it down to coals. Dress and draw the fish and place it into a Dutch oven, curving it around to fit with the belly side in. Cover with milk and bury the Dutch oven in the coals for 2 hours. (Keep the fire going, too.) While waiting, mix a stuffing with bread crumbs, celery, tarragon, salt, and black pepper. Remove the Dutch oven, carefully remove the lid, and carefully stuff the body cavity with the bread and celery mixture. Pour the wine over the fish. Return the lid and rebury in hot coals, adding more coals if needed, and cook for another 45 minutes. Enjoy hot.

Pine Bark Stew (p. 79)

8

Catfish and Bullheads

Skillet Cats, Pine Bark Stew, Flathead Jerky, and Other Tasty Recipes for a Mid-American Favorite

Some of my best catfish eating, or at least the most enjoyable, has been at old riverside fish camps. Many of these rustic joints featured "all you can eat" at a very reasonable price, and they really piled fish on the board, not on platters or plates but on grease-stained brown bags. These were usually small channel catfish—6 to 9 inches long—that were caught in fish baskets by local commercial fishermen. My guess is that the fishermen sold the small ones to the fish camp undressed. Then they filleted the larger ones for the market. On a few occasions, I have eaten fish camp cats no longer than 5 inches—some of which were fried in the skin. Almost always these were channel catfish, easily identified by their forked tail and sleek, speckled bodies. For some reason, the small channel cats were easier than other species to catch in large numbers in wire or wood slat baskets. Much depended on a good swift-water set.

A few of these fish camps still exist, but these days you are more likely to be fed farmed catfish, partly because commercial cat fishermen are now a rare breed and don't cotton to modern government regulation and red tape. Some of the farmed pond cats are good. Others are not so good. This can be a matter of texture. So . . . don't swallow hook, line, and sinker the common pitch from commercial catfish farmers and fish mongers. River cats don't taste muddy, unless the diner has a bad case of what I call mud on the mind. But, to be sure, some wild catfish available to the American angler are better than others. Note, however, that there is no such fish as a "mudcat." That term, unfortunately, became something of a mindset years ago, partly because some influential outdoor writers confused the bullhead (which was often the fish they caught during their youth from local ponds) with some of the other cats and better bullheads. In short, the bullhead, a sort of ugly duckling of the catfish world, deserves, like Rodney Dangerfield, more respect, culinarily speaking.

Moreover, the catfish is much more than a Southern specialty. It has always been popular in mid-America, thanks to the Mississippi River and its tributaries. In short, the catfish is as American as Huckleberry Finn.

The angler, as well as the chef and the diner, should also know that most catfish are not bottom feeders. The channel cat prefers swift water—and it often feeds on top. They will hit artificial lures, especially at night. The large flathead feeds primarily on hand size bluegill and similar sunfish— hardly a bottom-feeding scavenger as often implied. The large blue cat does feed extensively on the bottom, mostly because that's where the crawfish are. Some of the bullheads do feed on bottom, but that doesn't automatically give them a "muddy" taste.

Dozens of catfish species are known to ply the rivers and lakes of the Amazon basin of South America, including several giants. These include the tiger sorubim, spotted sorubim, and barred sorubim. Excellent eating, these are certainly not bottom feeders, for they actively hunt small fish to eat and will readily hit top-water plugs intended for peacock bass. Also, a huge Asian catfish that plies the Mekong is known as freshwater shark, and in Africa one species of catfish is definitely not a bottom feeder. It fact, it feeds exclusive on the surface—and swims upside-down to do so. So . . . it's high time for Americans to get mud off the mind and enjoy the plentiful catfish.

Of course, some of the catfish and bullheads are better than others. Here's my top-ten list—with which some anglers will surely take issue, and hotly so.

A.D.'s Top Ten North American Cats

1. Small Channel Cat, River Run. These are the favorites of discriminating Southern connoisseurs. They are caught in swift water, and can sometimes be taken in large numbers on light tackle. The channel cat is native to mid-America, from the Great Lakes south to the Gulf of Mexico. It has been introduced east and west of its original range. They grow up to 60 pounds or so, but the smaller ones are better for frying. The small ones have forked tails and spots on the side.

2. White Catfish. This is one of the best fish that swims. It is found mostly in coastal streams from Chesapeake Bay to Florida and Texas. It's a small fish, seldom growing over 3 pounds. The white is not as nocturnal as the other cats, and it often feeds by day. Because of its feeding habits and excellent flesh (firm and white), it is an excellent choice for pay-to-fish ponds. It's a good fish for kids to catch—and eat.

3. Larger River Run Channel Cat. All these are good, but the small ones are better. Of course, they also grow in large impoundments through which rivers run.

4. Large Flathead Catfish. These fierce predators live in streams and grow to 100 pounds. Their original range was the Mississippi Valley south into Mexico. Flatheads have been introduced to other areas, such as Florida, where some anglers cuss 'em because they think they'll eat all the bluegills and shellcrackers. (Some Florida people consider the flathead a trash fish!) In any case, the fish is very good, and, oddly, the large ones are considered just as good as, or even better than, the small ones.

5. Small Blue Catfish. These are almost as good as small channel catfish. They are not quite as sleek, and do not have forked tails and speckled bodies.

6. Large Blue Catfish. These also grow big, up to 100 pounds or better. This species is the largest of the North American catfish, and is often taken in large impoundments. It originally lived in rivers from Minnesota to Mexico, but it has been established east and west. It is usually found over bottoms of bedrock, sand, rocks, or gravel—hardly a "mudcat"! They make excellent eating. Try blue cat steaks on the grill, basted with Zesty Italian dressing.

7. Farmed Catfish. Once again . . . the angler has the best of the eating. Farm ponds and pay-to-fish ponds, in which the angler usually pays by the pound, can provide some fast action and make an excellent way to introduce kids to fishing. (During a feeding spree, these catfish readily take fly-rod popping bugs.) Once again, the angler will know that his fish are very fresh as compared to farmed fish that have run through the distribution chain.

Generally, these open-pond fish are better, and have a firmer and leaner flesh, than those raised in baskets for the markets. They are also happier.

8. White-Fleshed Bullheads. A number of bullheads make excellent eating. In my neck of the woods, a bullhead called "butter cat" is highly prized by some of the locals. I have eaten hundreds of them without ever knowing the scientific name of the species.

The yellow bullhead is not at all bad if eaten very fresh; ice your catch soon, otherwise its flesh will become rather mushy. This is not bad advice for any of the bullheads.

9. Saltwater Catfish. The gafftopsail saltwater catfish, so named because of its sail-like dorsal fin, is good eating, but most people release them—or throw them onto the bank to rot. What a waste. Gafftopsails are often caught in brackish water, or far up rivers that empty into salt water. The smaller sea cat is also good eating, and it too can be taken in brackish or fresh water.

10. Red-Fleshed Bullheads and Hybrids. As a general rule, those bullheads with white flesh are much better table fare than those with red. (The reverse is true with the trouts.) Some hybrid cats, which occur naturally, also have red flesh and are not of the best eating. Generally, these should be cooked in a stew instead of being fried. The local names of the various bullheads don't mean very much, and many people lump all of them in the term "mudcat." The color of the flesh is the best guide.

In addition to those listed above, there are some regional fish, such as the delicious Yaqui cat of northern Mexico and southern Arizona. The headwater catfish lives in northeastern Mexico up to the Pecos River system in Texas. The stonecat is another edible regional fish. Growing up to 12 inches in length, it prefers rocky streams, ranging from Montana to the Great Lakes, south to Texas.

So . . . there you have it. A top-ten list with lots of "ifs, ands, and buts." Here are a few culinary suggestions.

Bullhead Casserole

This dish can be cooked with any good catfish, such as the large flathead, and it is especially useful for cooking bullheads that may be a little questionable. The fish can be cooked in any way, including frying, but I suggest poaching the whole fish in a court bouillon (recipe in chapter 16). Poach the fish whole, cool, and flake off the meat with a fork.

- 1 ½ pounds flaked bullhead
- 8-ounce package egg noodles
- 1 can condensed cream of mushroom soup
- 2 tablespoons butter
- ½ cup half-and-half
- 1 cup shredded cheddar (preferably aged and hard)
- salt and black pepper to taste

Preheat the oven to 350 degrees. Cook the noodles by the directions on the package and put them into a buttered Pyrex casserole dish. Top with the fish flakes, spreading them evenly. In a bowl mix the rest of the ingredients except for the cheddar and add to the casserole, spreading it evenly with a spoon. Sprinkle the cheese on top and bake in the center of the oven for 30 minutes. If needed, turn on the broiler and brown the cheese nicely. Serve hot with a meal.

A.D.'s Pinwheel Steaks

Steaks cut from large catfish have a texture that is somehow quite different from a fillet cut from the same fish. The steaks are nice for broiling, and for grilling. They tend to be a little dry, so baste them from time to time.

The problem is in cutting the steaks across the backbone to a uniform thickness. It can be done at home, but an electric meat saw works better if you've got a friend at your local butcher's shop. If not, you might try my catfish pinwheels.

This method of making pinwheel steaks works with other large, long fish. The resulting steaks are easier to cut to uniform size, and the steaks have no backbones in them. Nice.

First you fillet the big cat. Lay the fillet out flat on a cutting board, skin-side down. Cut the middle half of the fillet into uniform 1-inch slices, saving the rib section and tail section for another use or for cooking as is. Place each 1-inch piece skin-side up and roll it from one end to the other. Wrap with a strip of bacon cut to length and pin with a round toothpick, as when preparing a filet mignon.

Rig for grilling or broiling at high heat. Baste the steaks heavily on both sides with bacon drippings kicked up with a few squirts of Tabasco sauce. Place the steaks about 6 inches above the coals or heat source. Cook for 5 or 6 minutes on each side, basting a time or two, or until the bacon is done enough to eat. Sprinkle with sea salt and serve up with mashed potatoes and vegetables or salad of your choice.

Broiled Catfish with Hollandaise

I love this simple recipe, using hollandaise sauce as a baste and as a table sauce. Make your own hollandaise (see chapter 16) or purchase some at the supermarket. The fillets should be about 1 inch thick.

2 pounds catfish fillets
hollandaise sauce
melted butter
salt and black pepper to taste

Preheat the broiler and a wide, shallow broiling pan. (The hot pan helps cook the fish without turning, but thick fillets should be broiled on both sides until done.) Flop the fillets in melted butter and sprinkle with salt and pepper. Arrange the fillets in the hot broiling pan. (Do not overlap.)

Broil about 4 inches from the heat source for 8 minutes. Using a tablespoon, spread hollandaise sauce rather heavily over each fillet. Broil for another 4 minutes, or until the sauce is bubbly. Serve with go-withs of your choice, along with lemon wedges and more hollandaise for those who can't get enough of the stuff.

Pine Bark Stew

Here's a catfish stew believed to have originated in North Carolina. No one is quite sure, but the name probably came about quite literally. The bark from felled pine trees can be peeled off in large curved pieces, which can be used to serve the stew in camp. If this derivation is correct, the stew should be quite thick so that it won't run out of either end of the bark.

2 pounds catfish fillets
¼ pound salt pork, diced
1 medium to large onion, diced
2 medium to large potatoes, diced
1 can chopped tomatoes (16-ounce size)
2 pods red pepper (hot) or pepper flakes
salt to taste
boiling water

Cook the salt pork in a stove-top Dutch oven until the oil renders out and the cracklings are crispy. Drain and reserve the cracklings. Add the onions to the pot and cook for 4 or 5 minutes, until they start to brown around the edges. Add the potatoes and red pepper, cover with spring water, bring to a boil, and simmer for 10 minutes, stirring a time or two with a wooden spoon. Add the diced tomatoes, along with the juice from the can. Serve the stew in bowls, or on pine bark, along with crackers or sopping bread. Sprinkle each serving with the reserved cracklings.

Catfish & Seafood Filé Gumbo

In spite of what might look like a long list of ingredients, this is an easy recipe as gumbo goes, designed for landlubbers who do not have a steady supply of fresh oysters, live crabs, and heads-on shrimp. The procedure can easily be adapted to these fresh ingredients, and, of course, the true Cajun will also insist that "first you make a roux." In any case, the gumbo is primarily a Southern dish, into the scheme of which catfish fillets fit nicely.

Of course, you will use the head and bony parts as part of the fish stock (which should also include shrimp heads and shells, crab shells, and oyster likker if you are using fresh seafood instead of canned). The filé used in the recipe can be purchased from most supermarkets these days, or you can make your own by grinding dried young sassafras leaves to a powder.

- 1 pound catfish fillets, cut into 1-inch cubes
- 1 pound canned shrimp (or cooked market shrimp)
- 1 pound canned crabmeat
- 1 pint of oysters with juice
- ¼ cup bacon drippings
- 1 large onion, chopped
- 1 green bell pepper, chopped
- 1 red bell pepper, chopped
- 1 jalapeño or cayenne pepper, seeded and chopped
- 2 ribs celery with green tops, chopped
- several scallions, chopped with about half of green tops
- 2 cups young okra, cut into wheels (frozen will do)
- 3 quarts fish stock (recipe in chapter 16)
- 3 cups chopped tomatoes
- 3 bay leaves
- salt and black pepper to taste
- 2 teaspoons filé
- fluffy white rice (cooked separately)

Heat the bacon drippings in a skillet and sauté the onion, peppers, celery, scallions, and okra for 10 minutes or so, stirring with a wooden spoon, until the onion is done.

Heat the fish stock with the bay leaves in a gumbo pot or large stove-top Dutch oven. Bring to a boil, add the catfish, and cook for 10 minutes. Add the skillet vegetables and the chopped tomatoes. Bring to a new boil. Add the shrimp and crab. Bring to a new boil. Add the oysters and oyster likker. Bring to a new boil. Cut off the heat and let the pot simmer while you cook the rice. (Note that the filé powder is not added to the boiling hot gumbo.)

To serve, ladle some gumbo into each partaker's bowl. Stir in a sprinkle of filé for those who want it. Then put a dollop of rice in the middle of each bowl, making a little mound. Serve immediately, along with some good, chewy French-style bread for sopping. Enjoy.

Brazilian Catfish Stew

Although catfish stew is usually associated with the southern United States, one kind or another is enjoyed in many other parts of the world. Here's a good one from Brazil, where dozens of species of catfish ply the Amazon and associated waterways.

The palm oil used in the recipe, although originally from Africa, is widely used in Brazil. It has a beautiful orange-gold color and a nutty flavor, both of which add to the stew. It can be purchased in Latin American and some other ethnic markets. If necessary, substitute bacon drippings.

I usually use jalapeños, but other hot peppers can also be used.

- 2 pounds catfish fillets
- 2 medium onions, chopped
- cloves garlic, chopped
- 3 medium tomatoes, chopped
- 2 fresh hot peppers, seeded and chopped
- 2 tablespoons chopped cilantro with roots (if available)
- ¼ cup lemon juice
- ¼ cup palm oil
- salt to taste

Cut the fillets into 2-inch squares and put into a large bowl. In a food processor or blender, zap the onions, garlic, tomatoes, peppers, and cilantro, with a little salt. Slowly pour in the lemon juice and blend until you have a smooth puree. Pour over the fish squares, mix with your hands, and let stand for an hour or a little longer.

Turn fish and sauce out into a saucepan. Carefully mix in ½ cup water and 1 tablespoon of the palm oil. Bring to heat, cover, and simmer for 10 minutes, until the fish flakes easily. Pour in the rest of the palm oil. Heat through. Turn out to a serving platter and surround with white rice, or ladle a serving of the stew into individual serving bowls and add a dollop of rice in the center. Enjoy with a chewy hot bread.

Go and catch another big river cat.

Redneck Newburg

A Newburg is a rich dish made up of crab or shrimp and a sauce of butter, cream, egg yolks, sherry, and so on. It is usually served over buttered toast points. So, this might not be a true Newburg—but it sure is good and it's easy to fix. Thank God for Campbell's soup. American cookery wouldn't be the same without it.

- 2 pounds catfish fillets
- 1 can cream of shrimp soup
- ½ cup dry sherry
- salt and pepper to taste
- rice (cooked separately)

Preheat the oven to 325 degrees. Sprinkle the fillets with salt and pepper. Arrange the fillets on a greased shallow baking pan. Heat the soup in a saucepan, stirring to prevent scorching on the bottom, and mix in the sherry. Pour the mixture over the fillets, spreading it evenly. Bake in the center of the oven for for 30 minutes, until the fish flakes easily when tested with a fork. Serve the fillets over a bed of rice, topped with the pan gravy. Feeds four.

Buttercat Soup with Avgolémono Sauce

Here in Northwest Florida where I live, we have a delicious little bullhead known as a butter cat. While living in a cabin on Dead Lakes for a few years, I caught and ate a sinful number of these fish. I ate them several days a week, and cast about for ways to cook them. Here is one of my favorites—a Greek-style soup. I usually made it in a stovetop Dutch oven, freezing any leftovers in small lunch-size containers.

Note that you can make the fish stock with the heads and backbones of the catfish. Also remember that the soup can be made with any good bullhead or catfish.

- 2 or 3 pounds catfish fillets
- 2 quarts fish stock (chapter 16)
- 4 large onions, sliced
- 4 large potatoes, peeled and diced
- 2 ribs celery with part of green tops, chopped
- 2 tablespoons olive oil
- 1 cup avgolémono sauce (recipe in chapter 16)
- salt and black pepper to taste

Heat the stock in a cast-iron Dutch oven. Add the onions, potatoes, and celery, olive oil, salt, and pepper. Bring to a boil, reduce the heat to a simmer, cover, and cook for 20 minutes. Cut the fillets into 1-inch cubes and add to the pot. Bring to a new boil, cover, and simmer for 15 minutes, until the fish flakes easily when tested with a fork. Stir in the avgolémono sauce. Serve hot with chewy Greek bread for sopping. This makes a good, filling supper for a cold night, so have plenty of bread to fill everybody up.

Catfish Hobo

Campers and backpackers don't need cooking utensils to fix a well-rounded fish dinner. A sheet of heavy-duty aluminum foil will do, and can be folded for easy carrying. Moreover, I suppose, it could be washed and used again, if need be. Of course, you should make a separate hobo packet for each person.

Although regular vegetables are used in this recipe, wild edibles can also be used, such as mushrooms, cattail shoots, catbrier heads, fiddleheads, and so on. There are dozens.

- bullhead fillets
- bacon
- potatoes, thinly sliced
- onion, sliced
- carrots (optional)
- green beans (optional)
- mushrooms, sliced
- tomatoes, sliced
- salt and pepper to taste

Open the aluminum foil on a flat surface. Cut a strip of bacon in half and position the halves in the center of the foil. Top with two bullhead fillets. Add thin layers of potatoes, onion, and other available vegetables. If you've got tomatoes, put them on top.

Make double folds in the foil all around, and punch a small vent hole in the top. Place packets directly on the hot coals, fish-side down, for 15 minutes. Turn over and cook for another 10 minutes. Carefully remove the packets from the fire, let cool, unfold at the top, and enjoy. If it isn't done, write me a nasty letter.

Flathead Jerky

Good jerky can be made with most fish, but I really prefer fish with mild white flesh. The larger flathead catfish are perfect, and the belly contains a slab of meat of uniform thickness, making it easy to cut jerky strips, rather like thick bacon. I like mine about ⅜ inch thick. The slab slices a little easier if you partly freeze it before cutting. A sharp knife helps.

A thousand recipes for a jerky marinade will work with catfish, and a simple soy sauce is great, perhaps helped along by a little black pepper and liquid smoke. Here's one of my favorite recipes.

flathead belly strips
salt
Tabasco sauce

Put the fish into a nonmetallic container and sprinkle generously with salt and lightly with Tabasco. Toss about with your hands, coating all sides. Arrange the strips in your dehydrator or in an oven with the door slightly ajar. Turn the heat up to 140 degrees and dry the fish for 6 hours or longer.

I eat these right away, some while still warm. If you have jerked a large flathead, longer storage may be needed. Simply put the strips in a mason jar and seal, or, better, seal them in a plastic bag with an electric vacuum pack system.

Note: If you live in a dry, windy place, the jerky strips can be dried on the clothesline. I tried this once using fish hooks to hold the jerky—and damn near caught my neighbor's dog.

The Sac à Lait Fry (p. 86)

Crappie

Cross Creek Crappie Cakes, Papermouth Pie, Blackened Crappie Fillets, with Notes on Salt-Curing Crappie and Other Fish

Primarily a fish of mid-America, the crappie has been stocked in other parts of the country. There are two kinds: white crappie and black crappie, but practical anglers don't worry about which is which. They look pretty much alike, act alike, and taste alike. Both species of crappie are called white perch, speckled perch, calico bass, strawberry bass, bachelor perch, sac à lait, papermouth, and so on, depending on region. Rednecks call them crap-pee, with emphasis on the "crap," whereas city slickers and more refined folk call them crop-pee.

The crappie is a fish of both lakes and streams, where it prefers sluggish water. It is attracted to cover, such as sumps, logs, docks, and so on. Most of the large man-made impoundments provide purely excellent habitat and plenty of food. Night fishing under a light or lantern with minnows is very popular in some areas, and can be very, very productive. Many anglers fish for crappie only during the spring pre-spawn schooling season, when they can catch enough to fill the freezer. Although most crappie by far are caught with minnows, they also take small spinners, such as the Rooster Tail, and streamer flies and bucktails that imitate minnows. Small jigs can also be productive.

As table fare, the crappie has a soft, mild white flesh that many people prefer over most other kinds of fish. Others prefer a firmer fish. In either camp, frying is by far the most popular way to cook crappie, either whole or filleted.

Easy to scale, the crappie can be pan-dressed or filleted. People who catch them for the freezer in large numbers usually fillet them to save freezer space. Normally, the fillets are frozen in water, which makes them keep well. The new home vacuum-pack systems also work well, and don't take as much freezer space. Because filleting wastes a lot of good flesh, I have included a few fish-flake recipes for the frugal angler. I have also added a couple of recipes that firm up the soft flesh, which, in my opinion, makes for better eating.

Most of the catch will be hand-size, but the crappie can grow up to five pounds. Large ones, called slabs, are unusual, however, and in many waters the fish are stunted from overpopulation. These should be caught and eaten without guilt. Any angler who releases them either doesn't like good fried fish or is simply too lazy to dress the catch.

The Sac à Lait Fry

Pecans and fried fish are popular in Louisiana, where the crappie is called sac à lait. Of course, any good breading can be used for the fry, including plain flour or cornmeal, but this one is special in Cajun country. If you are cooking whole crappies, a large deep-fryer is desirable, but a skillet will do for fillets.

4 pounds whole crappies or 2 pounds of fillets
1 cup cornmeal
1 cup pecan pieces (or pecan meal)
1 cup fresh bread crumbs
2 guinea hen eggs (or chicken eggs)
salt and cayenne to taste
oil for frying

In a food processor or blender, zap the pecans, cornmeal, and bread crumbs. Whisk the eggs lightly. Sprinkle the fish with salt and a little cayenne, then coat them with egg and dredge in the meal mixture. Rig for frying at 375 degrees. Fry the fish several pieces at a time until golden brown. Drain on absorbent paper. Serve Cajun Hush Puppies (recipe in chapter 16) and go-withs of your choice. I'll take a little fried okra with mine, and some of those sliced tomatoes.

Cross Creek Crappie Patties

Here's a recipe from Marjorie Kinnan Rawlings, author of *The Yearling*. She lived on Cross Creek in Florida, which connects Orange Lake and Lake Lockloosa. It is best made with diced crappie fillets, but flaked leftover fried crappie will also work.

2 cups crappie flakes or finely diced fillets
1 cup dry bread crumbs
½ cup milk
2 large chicken eggs, lightly beaten
2 tablespoons chopped fresh parsley
1 tablespoon Worcestershire sauce
salt and pepper to taste
butter

Roll up your sleeves. In a bowl mix all the stuff except the butter. Shape into patties. Heat the butter in a cast-iron skillet and sauté the patties for several minutes on each side, turning once with a a spatula. Serve for lunch with fried okra, sliced tomatoes, and so on.

Crappie Scrapple

Usually made with pork scraps or bony parts at hog killing time, this old recipe, still popular in Pennsylvania, can also be made with fish parts that are often thrown away. It is, therefore, a good recipe for those amongst our ranks who fillet crappie and throw out the heads and bones. The bony parts add to the scrapple. Of course, scrapple can also be made with other fish.

If you already have some leftover fish flakes and stock, you can skip the first part of the recipe.

1 cup fish flakes
1 ½ cups fine-ground white cornmeal
1 teaspoon grated onion
4 cups fish stock (as described in recipe directions, or use the recipe in chapter 16)
salt and black pepper to taste
¼ teaspoon sage
butter, cooking oil, or bacon drippings

Heat some water in a pot and add the fish heads and backbones, along with some chopped onion and celery. Bring to a boil and simmer until the fish flakes easily from the bone. Strain out the fish pieces, drain, and flake off the meat. Measure out enough fish flakes for the scrapple and save the rest for another meal.

Put the heads and bones back into the pot and cook at a very low boil to make a good fish stock. (Long cooking is best to render the magic from the bones.)

Mix the cornmeal, onion, and 4 cups of fish stock in a heavy pot, bring to a boil, then stir in the fish, salt, pepper, and sage. Cook and stir constantly until the mixture is thick. Ladle the mixture into a greased loaf pan or mold, then put it into the refrigerator to cool.

When you are ready to eat, slice the scrapple into ½-inch strips, roll in cornmeal, and fry in butter or oil until it is browned on both sides. I like to cook a strip or two of bacon on a griddle, then use bacon grease for cooking the scrapple.

Papermouth Pie

You'll need pastry for a 9-inch double-crust pie for this dish. Use your family recipe, or take the easy way out and buy frozen pastry at the supermarket. I like to cook this one with several rather small fillets, boneless and skinned.

½ pound crappie fillets
pastry for double-crust pie
1 ¼ cups cooked rice
2 hard-boiled chicken eggs
frozen stick of butter
1 tablespoon grated onion
1 tablespoon grated red bell pepper
salt and white pepper to taste

Preheat the oven to 400 degrees. Grease the pie pan and cover the bottom with pie dough. Add half the rice. Top with the crappie fillets. Grate the boiled eggs and sprinkle on top. Grate over the egg about ¼ stick of frozen butter. Add with the grated onion, grated bell pepper, and the rest of the rice. Sprinkle with salt and white pepper.

Top with the remaining pie crust. Crimp the edges with your finger and make a few slits on top with a knife. Bake in the center of the oven for 45 minutes, until the crust browns lightly. Turn off the oven heat and let the pie coast a little before serving.

George Foreman Crappie Fillets

I love to cook fish fillets in a George Foreman Grilling Machine, or one of the several similar gadgets on the market. Since these heat from the top and bottom, like an electric waffle iron, they do a quick job—and, I think, are much better than a microwave. The grill marks add to the flavor.

This "recipe" is really more of a cooking method, and variations are endless. I use fish sauce here because the crappie is a very bland fish that can stand a little enhancement. The fish sauce, usually Thai or Vietnamese, is available in Asian markets and, these days, in a lot of supermarkets, as it damn well should be.

If you don't care for fish sauce, try soy sauce, stir-fry sauce, or some such Asian concoction. Most of these will not require salt, but some "low-sodium" sauces will be improved by a little salt. Also, try swabbing the fillets with mayonnaise, or smear on a thin layer of tomato-based salsa, mild or hot, as you like it. A mixture of melted butter and lemon juice is also very good.

Of course, you can also sprinkle on all manner of spices, dill weed, and so on. If you want to eat Greek, baste the fillets on both sides with olive oil that has been infused with garlic and sprinkle on a little oregano.

So . . . you see the possibilities. When you dress and freeze your crappie catch, consider freezing some of the fillets singly and wrap them separately in plastic film or seal in a vacuum bag. That way, you can get out exactly what you need.

The Grilling Machine and a batch of frozen fillets can provide many an impromptu lunch. What could be better? What quicker?

crappie fillets, skinless (frozen or fresh)
Pam no-stick spray
fish sauce

When you are ready to cook, preheat the grilling machine. Spray the grill surface with Pam, or grease it with cooking oil, to help prevent sticking. If you are using fresh fillets, put them on the bottom grill and squirt on some fish sauce. Close the grill and cook for 5 minutes. (Small fillets will take only 4 minutes, and those over an inch thick will take a little longer.) The fish is done when it flakes easily when tested with a fork. If sticking is a problem, run a slim table knife blade up the channels. Serve hot with whatever you like with grilled fish.

If the fillets are frozen, double the cooking time. Cook for 5 minutes, then open the grill and squirt on the sauce. Cook for another 5 minutes.

Blackened Crappie Fillets

Blackened redfish became something of a culinary fad a few years ago. The recipe—or cooking method—is commonly attributed to Louisiana chef Paul Prudhomme. When properly done, it has a spicy crust that is unique, but, unfortunately, too many modern versions, including those served in many restaurants, are rather soggy.

The trick is to coat the fillets with blackening dust and sear them quickly on a very, very hot cast-iron griddle or in a skillet. There will be some smoke, so don't try this in the kitchen unless you have a very good vent over your stove.

Some of the Cajun recipes for blackening powder have a long list of ingredients, but some of this stuff is not necessary. The key to success is in having lots of mild paprika or ancho chile powder in the mix. (A lot of the so-called paprika sold in our markets is really made from dried red ancho or New Mexico chiles.) This allows you to have a very thick coating that isn't too hot to eat. If you like fiery foods, however, you may want to cut back on the mild pepper. Incidentally, many of the commercial blackening dusts on the market can be diluted by the addition of more mild paprika or ancho. (Try Pendery's in Texas, or google the Internet. Remember also that the ancho powder is a purely excellent filler to add to commercial chili powder. It gives your chili a nice red color, flavor, and sustenance not available with ordinary chili powders.)

For success, the technique should be used with thin fillets. (For this reason, Prudhomme's original recipe called for small redfish, and the fad quickly depleted the supply.) Crappie fillets are flat and work perfectly. Note that using a thick fillet will cause the outside to burn too badly before the inside gets done. I like the fillets to be half an inch thick. If they are slightly thicker in the middle, I flatten them lightly with a wooden mallet.

Although I find that the size and shape of crappie fillets work nicely for blackening, other fish can be used—if they are not too thick.

Try a few just for the hell of it. Then cook up a batch whenever you are feeding culinary sports who like hot stuff.

- crappie fillets, skinless and boneless
- ½ cup red ancho chile powder
- 1 tablespoon cayenne (or to taste)
- 1 tablespoon black pepper
- 1 tablespoon white pepper
- 1 tablespoon fine sea salt
- 1 tablespoon onion powder
- melted butter

Mix all the spices and spread out in a wide bowl or deep plate and set aside. Heat a cast-iron skillet or a flat griddle on high heat until it is as hot as you can get it. That's right. Do not put any grease or butter on the surface of the skillet or griddle. If you do, you'll have a burnt smell and lots of smoke. (Don't worry. The fish is not going to stick to the surface. Anyone who advises you to grease the griddle or skillet is misguided.)

While the griddle is heating, flip-flop the fillets in the spice mix and set aside. Then, one at a time, turn the fillets in melted butter and flip-flop them once again in the spice mixture. Set aside for a few minutes until you do the whole batch.

If the griddle is hot enough, carefully lay a coated fillet on it. (I use good tongs for this.) Let it sizzle for half a minute. Then turn it and sizzle the other side for half a minute. Set it on a serving platter and do another one. This procedure gives you a tasty fillet that is charred and crispy on the outside and moist and white inside.

Serve with vegetables of your choice, a chef's salad, and some good bread. Beer or iced tea hits the spot.

Salted Crappie

This technique of salting fish has been adapted from my book *Cold-Smoking and Salt-Curing Meat, Fish, & Game,* which contains other useful information and international recipes for salt fish, which, before mechanical refrigeration, was a very important staple in many parts of the world.

I discuss the subject in this chapter because crappie are often caught in large numbers and because the salt cure makes the flesh a little firmer and more toothsome. In short, I find that salting is a good alternative to freezing your catch. Also note that salting can be done at home or in camp, or even in a boat.

To dress the crappie, you can simply cut a fillet off either side, leaving the head and backbone for soup or stock. For a much quicker method, butterfly the fish without scaling. Then the fish can be salted in one piece. (Mullet are dressed this way for salting or smoking in large numbers.) It's very quick. Behead the fish and cut down the backbone toward the head. Do not cut through the belly. The innards are easy to remove. (This is also a good way to roe a fish. Cutting in from the top is less likely to puncture the roe sacs.) Note that the fish does not have to be scaled at this time. Rinse and drain the fish.

Find enough large nonmetallic containers (such as plastic or styrofoam ice chests). Put a layer of salt in the bottom. Also put some salt into a small shallow plastic tray or other container. Lay a crappie fillet or whole butterflied crappie in the shallow salt container, then turn it to coat the other side. Pick it up by the tail, bringing out as much salt as sticks on it. Layer the fish, scales-down, in the large container. Sprinkle on a layer of salt, add another layer of fish, and so on until the container is almost full. The last layer should be put in skin-side up, with plenty of salt piled on top.

Cover the container and store it in a cool place for a week. A basement or garage will do. A brine will develop as the salt draws the moisture out of the fish, making them shrink in size and become firmer.

After a week, remove the fish and discard the brine. Make a new brine by boiling some water and adding salt until the solution will float an egg. While the new brine is hot, add a few peppercorns if you want them. Cool the brine. Put the fish back into the container and pour the cooled brine over them. Put a nonmetallic weight of some sort, such as a block of wood, on top of the fish to keep them submerged and unexposed to the air. Cover the container with a cloth and leave it in a cool place for 2 weeks.

After 2 weeks, the fish can be freshened (soaked in fresh water) and cooked by a variety of recipes, or they can be stored until needed. They can also be washed, packaged, and frozen.

You can also hang the fish in the wind and sun if you have a suitable place without cats, dogs, and coons. Try a few on the clotheline, but take them in when it rains.

Note also that the salt-curing process will, in time, also soften the bones in such fish as suckers. Note also that the salt cure is often followed by smoking.

To fry salt-cured crappie, a day ahead of the meal "freshen" the fish by soaking them in fresh water all night, perhaps changing the water a time or two. Then you can dust them with meal or flour and fry them in hot oil as usual. They will need no salt or other seasoning. When you are ready to cook, drain the fish, dust them in flour or fine meal, and fry them in hot oil as usual. Note that the fish will need no salt or seasoning.

This might well be the best crap-pee or crop-ee you'll ever enjoy—and salting is the key.

Perch

Perch Parmesan, Thai Perch Patties, Vermont Hard Cider Perch, along with Arguments for the Best Fish Chowder

I don't have space or time to argue here at length with irate Texans who will want to include the Rio Grande perch, a small sunfish, in this chapter, or with many old-timers who still call the crappie white perch. In chapter 5, I have already taken on a West Coast outdoor foods writer who confused, in a big way, the white bass with the white perch, and I can't restrain the devil in me who wants to sting the New York fish-and-game cooking columnist who referred to "a fatty fish like the perch." The perch fatty? Turns out he was talking about the ocean perch, a large seagoing fish that is not taken by sportsmen but is common in New York's Fulton Fish Market. This guy didn't even speak the angler's lingo, and apparently the editors of the magazine didn't either. He's the one, by the way, who said the angler who thinks he can go out and catch a better fish than he can buy is kidding himself! We know better.

Anyhow, I'll cut through a lot of piscatory confusion concerning the naming of fish. The perch I'm talking about in this chapter include only the white perch *(Morone americana)* and the yellow perch *(Perca flavescens)*. This is, I admit, a somewhat arbitrary classification, and sports west of the Rockies might make a case for the Sacramento perch, a rather large sunfish that can weigh almost 10 pounds.

The white perch lives primarily in the Northeast, ranging from Nova Scotia to North Carolina and west to the Great Lakes. It can be caught in fresh, brackish, and, sometimes, even in salt water. In profile, the white perch looks somewhat like the striped bass, to which they are related. In weight they average about a pound. There are lots of 'em, and they are often taken with the fly rod. Best of all, when eaten fresh and properly cooked, white perch will hold their own with anything in the fishmonger's bill of fare. Their firm white flesh is good cooked by any method, and it makes a purely excellent New England fish chowder.

The yellow perch provides fast action and very good eating in the Midwest and east to the Atlantic drainage. During my lifetime, it has expanded its range southward all the way to Florida. Although the yellow perch grows up to 2 pounds or better, the average is ½ pound or less. In some waters they may be somewhat stunted owing to overpopulation. These fish should be caught and eaten, and they can be taken day or night, and through the ice. Around the Great Lakes, the fish is sometimes available commercially from Lake Erie.

The flesh is firm and white, but it can become a little tough if overcooked. The small ones are better in the skillet.

In any case, here are a few recipes to try for both white and yellow perch.

Perch Salad (p. 95)

Perch Parmesan

This is a wonderful dish that is best cooked with a small, long fish, such as the yellow perch. Scale and gut the fish, but leave the heads on. This recipe can easily be adapted for larger fish and fillets.

- 2 pounds small yellow perch
- olive oil
- 2 cloves garlic, finely minced
- 1 ½ cups finely grated hard Parmesan
- 1 cup Italian bread crumbs (seasoned)
- sea salt

Preheat the oven to 400 degrees. Mix the olive oil and garlic in an oblong baking pan and marinate the fish for 10 minutes, turning to coat all sides. Remove the fish and roll in a mixture of the cheese and bread crumbs. Arrange the fish in a single layer in a shallow baking pan, well greased. Bake for 12 minutes, or until the fish flakes easily when tested with a fork.

White Perch Meuniere

This famous old French recipe, which means "miller's wife," works nicely for white perch fillets. Unlike many French recipes, a simple sauce is made directly in the skillet in which the fish is cooked.

- 2 pounds perch fillets, boneless
- ½ cup butter
- salt and pepper to taste
- all-purpose flour from the miller
- juice of 1 lemon
- 1 tablespoon chopped fresh parsley

Melt the butter in a skillet on low heat. Sprinkle the fillets on both sides with salt and pepper, then dust lightly with flour. A few at a time, sauté the fillets over medium heat until lightly browned on both sides. Don't let the butter burn, and add more as needed. Remove the fish to a heated serving platter. Stir the lemon juice and parsley into the pan drippings. Cook for several minutes, stirring as you go. Pour the sauce over the fish and serve.

Vermont Hard-Cider Perch

I have always been a fan of hard cider. In my opinion, it beats beer for drinking—and wine for cooking. Bottled hard cider is available these days in the beer section of supermarkets and liquor stores.

- 6 white perch fillets
- ½ cup butter
- chopped fresh parsley
- salt and black pepper to taste
- bread crumbs
- 1 cup hard cider

Preheat the oven to 350 degrees. Melt the butter in a Pyrex baking pan or dish suitable for serving. Sprinkle in some parsley. Arrange the fillets in the pan, side by side, and sprinkle with salt and pepper. Brush or drizzle on the butter, evenly. Sprinkle with bread crumbs, and some more parsley. Add the hard cider and bake in the center of the over for 10 minutes, or until the fish flakes easily when tested with a fork.

Easy Perch Pie

Here's a good one to feed people who think they don't like fish. White perch are recommended, but any good mild fish will work. It can be made with leftovers from fried, broiled, poached or baked fish.

Preheat the oven to 350 degrees. Grease a baking dish with butter and add a layer of mashed potatoes. Spread on a layer of fish flakes. Then a layer of finely chopped onions. Top with a layer of mashed potatoes and cook in the center of the oven for 30 minutes. Sprinkle with a little mild paprika and serve.

Yellow Perch Dog

I like to make this with hollow perch fillets and regular hot dog buns. Use skinless fillets. With small perch, use two fillets per dog, crossed lengthwise in the bun. Also try these dogs with fried fish fillets.

To proceed, rig for steaming, preferably using a large bamboo steamer rig. When the water is boiling, steam the fillets until they flake easily when tested with a fork. Carefully remove the fillets.

Turn down the heat and put the hot dog buns into the steamer for a few minutes. You want the buns warm and moist, but not soggy. Slather each bun with homemade mayonnaisc (see recipe in chapter 16). Add a steamed fillet and smear on a little more mayonnaise.

There you have it. Kids love this dog. Of course, you can use catsup, mustard, pickle relish, and so on. Even sauerkraut. But plain steamed fish and mayonnaise is hard to beat.

Deluxe Perch Dog

This is a heartier version of the basic dog recipe, served with a chunky fish gravy.

When dressing the perch, set the fillets aside and put the heads and bony parts into a pot with some water and chopped celery. Bring to a boil and simmer for 15 minutes or so. Fish out the backbones and pull off the meat. Then do the heads the same way.

Put the bones back into the pot and boil down to a rich stock. Salt and pepper to taste. Remove half a cup of the stock and stir in 2 or 3 tablespoons of flour. Stir back into the main pot, making a thin gravy. Stir in the reserved fish flakes and cook a little longer, making a chunky gravy, to be used like chili on a regular dog. Keep warm.

Next, cook the fillets and prepare the fish dogs according to the previous recipe. (Use the mayonnaise sparingly.) Top with the gravy and enjoy.

New England Perch Rolls

This is a delicious dish, not unlike an old-time New England lobster roll, that is a cut above your average modern-day sub sandwich.

- 1 pound white perch fillets
- flour
- 4 hero buns
- Homemade Mayonnaise (recipe in chapter 16)
- prepared mustard
- 1 medium Vidalia onion, chopped
- 2 gherkins, minced
- 1 large tomato, peeled and chopped
- 1 chicken egg, lightly whisked
- oil for frying
- 1 or 2 tablespoons melted butter
- salt, black pepper, and mild paprika

Preheat the oven to 350 degrees and rig for frying in a skillet. Cut the fillets in half lengthwise (to make them fit nicely into the roll). Salt and pepper the fillets. Roll in egg and shake in flour. Quickly fry, a few at a time, until golden brown. Set aside to drain.

Split the rolls in half and scoop out the soft centers. Mix the mayonnaise, mustard, onion, and minced gherkin in a bowl. Spread the mixture on each half of the rolls. Fill the center of the roll halves with fried fish fillets. Spoon the chopped tomatoes over the fish fillets. Press the halves together as best you can. Brush all around with melted butter. Wrap in aluminum foil and bake for 15 minutes in the center of the oven. Remove the foil and serve hot or warm on a plate. Eat out of hand, but have a fork ready if needed.

Perch Salad

I love a good fish salad for a light lunch, and this is one of my favorites.

- 2 pounds boneless white perch fillets
- 1 cup Homemade Mayonnaise (recipe in chapter 16)
- ½ cup minced onion
- ½ cup minced celery with green tops
- ¼ cup minced red bell pepper
- ¼ cup minced green bell pepper
- ¼ cup minced radishes
- 2 tablespoons minced scallion tops (optional)
- 2 tablespoons minced gherkin
- 2 hard-boiled chicken eggs, chopped
- juice and zest of 1 lemon
- salt and pepper to taste
- lettuce leaves for serving

Poach the fillets for 10 minutes. Drain and cut into ¾-inch cubes. Using your hands, mix the rest of the ingredients in a bowl and gently mix in the fish chunks. Serve on lettuce leaves, along with crackers or bread, for a light lunch.

Thai Perch Patties with Fish Sauce

This recipe calls for Thai fish sauce, which can, fortunately, be found in ethnic markets and in most upscale supermarkets these days. Substitute Vietnamese fish sauce if need be, or any other Asian fish sauce. This is good stuff, quite similar to the garnum treasured by the ancient Roman culinary sports.

If you want a taste of Southeast Asia, be sure to try this recipe. In addition to being full of flavor, it is also highly nutritious. Leftover perch can be used, or poach and flake a few before proceeding.

1 ½ to 2 cups poached perch flakes
1 tablespoon flour
4 chicken eggs, lightly whisked
2 scallions with about half the green tops, minced
2 or 3 tablespoons Thai fish sauce
¼ teaspoon black pepper
peanut oil

Spread the flaked fish out on a surface, and sprinkle the flour over it. Then put the floured fish into a bowl and stir in the whisked eggs, minced scallion, fish sauce, and pepper. Heat a little peanut oil in a skillet, then ladle or quickly spoon in about ¼ of the fish mixture and spread it out. Cook until the bottom is browned, then flip the patty over and brown the other side. Repeat the procedure with the rest of the mixture.

These patties look like flapjacks and can be stacked for hungry eaters. Have a little Vietnamese Nuoc Cham sauce (recipe in chapter 16) for dipping.

The Skillet Fry

Scale the perch and cut out the fin spines before cooking. Then eat them like corn on the cob, pulling the meat off the backbone with your teeth.

8 or 10 small perch
1 cup finely crushed saltines
½ cup cornmeal
corn oil
½ cup half-and-half
salt and freshly ground black pepper to taste
lemon wedges (for garnish)

Mix the cornmeal, cracker crumbs, salt, and pepper in a shake bag. Dip the fish into the half-and-half, then shake them in the crumb mixture, being sure to coat inside and out. Set aside.

Heat ¾ inch of oil in a deep skillet, getting it hot enough to spit back at you. Fry the fish for 3 or 4 minutes on each side, until golden brown and crisp. Do not overcrowd the skillet, frying in several batches. Remove the fish to drain on a brown bag or twice-folded paper towels. Serve hot, along with lemon wedges, baked beans, cole slaw, or whatever you want with your fried fish. Personally, I like to pig out on fried perch, french fries, and fried hush puppies, along with sliced tomato and sliced Vidalia onions.

Macadamia Perch Fillets

Native to Australia, the macadamia nut is now available from farms in Hawaii and California. If you buy them in the shell, make sure you have a hammer to crack them with.

- 2 pounds perch fillets
- ¾ cup melted butter
- ¾ cup chopped macadamia nuts
- sea salt and freshly ground black pepper

Preheat the oven to 375 degrees. Sprinkle the fillets on both sides with salt and pepper. Grease a shallow baking pan suitable for serving. Place the fish in the pan in a single layer but tightly packed. Mix the nuts into the melted butter and pour evenly over the fish. Bake in the center of the oven for 20 minutes. Turn on the broiler heat and broil for a few minutes to brown the nuts lightly. Serve hot with a good bread, steamed asparagus or other vegetable, and a Hawaiian fruit salad.

Colonial Fish Soup

This soup was often cooked at the fireplace during Colonial times, using shellfish as well as fish. The recipe can be varied quite a bit, depending on what you have on hand. Cook it in your fireplace if you are rigged with a pot that can be swung in and out. It also works nicely in a large stove-top cast-iron Dutch oven.

The recipe calls for fish stock, which can be made with the heads, backbones, and rib cages of the white perch along with shrimp heads and shells. (To make the stock, see recipe in chapter 16.) Allspice replaced mace, nutmeg, and cloves in frugal recipes—and it still works. For full flavor, use whole allspice berries and grind them in your mortar and pestle. Note that in this recipe the salt pork is not browned in the pot.

- 3 pounds perch fillets cut into 1-inch cubes
- 1 cup salt pork, finely diced
- 1 pound shucked oysters (small)
- 1 pound peeled shrimp
- 1 quart combined fish stock (recipe in chapter 16) and oyster juice
- 3 cups diced potatoes
- 6 tomatoes, quartered
- 2 medium to large onions, diced
- 10 scallions with part of green tops, diced
- ½ cup diced cucumber
- ½ cup chopped fresh parsley
- 1 cup butter
- water (about a quart)
- zest of 1 lemon
- 1 tablespoon freshly ground allspice
- flour
- salt and black pepper to taste
- 3 cups cooked noodles or rice (optional)

Salt and pepper the fish and dredge in flour. Heat the butter in the pot and brown the fish. Remove to drain. In the remaining butter, brown the onions. Pour in the fish stock and heat to a light boil. Add the potatoes, tomatoes, salt pork, allspice, cucumbers, and lemon zest. Cook for 15 minutes. Add the shrimp for 6 minutes, following with reserved fish and the oysters. Cook until the oysters curl around the edges. Add the cooked noodles or rice if wanted as a filler or thickener. (Add some water if you want a thinner soup.) Serve hot in bowls, along with plenty of good bread and a lemon wedge in each bowl. Hunker down and fill up.

New England Fish Chowder

This old dish goes back to the seafaring days of New England, when the cod trade was very important. It was often made with salt cod as well as fresh. Pollock and other saltwater fish are used. Freshwater fish also work, and the white perch is pretty nigh perfect. (L.L. Bean, in his early camping book, also gave a nod to the black bass, probably with smallmouth in mind.)

Some of the better chowders are made by jackleg cooks who don't follow a written recipe—yet, they will raise hell if you deviate from the standard ingredients. Further, I understand it's against the law in the state of Maine to put tomatoes into anything called chowder. Most modern versions use plain water, but the frugal cook will surely take the trouble to make a good stock from the fish heads and bony parts.

In any case, my recipe is based on one set forth in the *Boston Cooking School Cook Book* back in 1884. The book calls for "butter crackers," and I'm not sure what these are. Some modern New Englanders look for "chowder crackers," which are not widely available. Oyster crackers are commonly used in chowder, and are listed here because they are so widely available. In all good conscience, however, I can't let the subject go without saying that the original New England chowder—the world's best—is made with old-time hardtack layered in with the fish and potatoes.

A female book editor once reminded me rather strongly that she was born and raised in New England and had never heard of anybody layering the hardtack in the chowder. Instead, it was crumbled and served on top. Well . . . she had a hand in this book and she's still after me on this point!

- 5 pounds white perch fillets
- 2-inch cube of salt pork, diced
- 6 Maine potatoes, sliced
- several small onions
- 1 quart hot milk
- 1 tablespoon melted butter
- salt and white pepper to taste
- fish stock (recipe in Chapter 16)

Cut the fatty salt pork into small dice, about ¼-inch. Fry it in a skillet until you have rendered oil and crisp cracklings. Remove and save the cracklings. Brown the onions in the pork fat, drain, and save.

Pour the fat into a pot or stove-top Dutch oven, preferably cast-iron. Bring to heat and add the sliced potatoes. Cover with fish stock (use water if you must). Add the reserved onions, fish chunks, salt, and pepper. Cover and simmer for 10 minutes or so, or until the fish is done.

Add the butter and hot milk. Stir and take off the heat. Serve hot, ladling the chowder into serving bowls. Serve oyster crackers (or chowder crackers, crumbled, if you have them) to be used as wanted by each partaker. Also ration out the reserved cracklings to be used as an optional topping.

Manhattan Fish Chowder

The Manhattan fish chowder is much lighter and less filling than an authentic New England fish chowder. The main difference is that the modern Manhattan version contains no milk, butter, or salt pork. It does contain tomatoes, which lighten up the chowder and make it more attractive. In general the Manhattan chowder is considered more of an appetizer, whereas the New England chowder is a heavy, rib-sticking hot meal for a cold New England night.

- 4 nice white perch
- 2 medium potatoes, peeled and diced
- 4 cups diced fresh tomato (peeled)
- 1 medium onion, diced
- ½ cup minced celery with part of green tops
- ¼ cup minced bell pepper
- 1 clove garlic, minced
- 1 tablespoon minced fresh parsley
- 3 tablespoons olive oil
- salt and freshly ground black pepper to taste
- 2 bay leaves

Scale and fillet the white perch. Cut the fillets into 1-inch chunks and set aside. Put the heads and bony parts into a pot or stove-top Dutch oven. Cover (barely) with water and add the bay leaves. Bring to a boil, cover, and simmer for 15 minutes or so. Using a slotted spoon, remove the fish pieces, being sure to get all the bones. Drain and flake off the meat with a fork, putting it back into the pot and discarding the bones. Heat the olive oil in a skillet and sauté the onion, bell pepper, and garlic for a few minutes, stirring with a wooden spoon as you go. Add the skillet contents to the pot, along with the tomatoes, potatoes, celery, parsley, salt, and black pepper. Stir to mix everything, then gently stir in the fish chunks. Simmer for 15 minutes. Serve hot in bowls, along with crackers or perhaps a chewy French bread.

Broiled Yellow Perch Italian

Small yellow perch, dressed whole, line up nicely in a broiling pan. Any good basting sauce, such as lemon butter (recipe in chapter 16), will do, but bottled Italian dressing from the supermarket is hard to beat. Perch of 7 to 9 inches are perfect for broiling.

- 12 small yellow perch
- olive oil
- flour
- Italian salad dressing
- salt and black pepper
- coarsely grated hard Parmesan
- Italian parsley (garnish)

Brush the fish with olive oil and shake in a flour bag. Let sit for 20 minutes or so. While waiting, preheat the broiler. Line the dusted perch up in a well-greased shallow broiling pan. The sides can be touching if need be. Brush the perch lightly with Italian salad dressing and sprinkle with a little salt and pepper.

Place the pan about 4 inches under the heat source. Broil for 4 minutes. Turn, baste, sprinkle lightly with Parmesan cheese, and broil for 4 minutes, or until the cheese begins to brown and the fish flake easily when tested with a fork. Serve hot with vegetables, salad, and Italian bread. If you are serving guests, garnish with parsley—and open a bottle of paisano.

Fish Gumbo

Well, now that we have stirred up all the New Yorkers and upper New England Yankees, we might as well tick off all the rednecks and Cajuns. Truth is, perch fillets go nicely in a seafood gumbo. I might add that this is a quick recipe. Note that I have omitted the filé. The okra, however, is essential for a gumbo, and most food writers and even a few Cajun cooks need to know this fact. The very word "gumbo" comes from similar African words meaning "okra." Omit it at your culinary peril. It is essential to the texture of a gumbo.

- 4 cups small shrimp, peeled
- 4 cups diced perch
- 1 cup lard plus more as needed
- 4 cups young okra cut into ¾-inch wheels
- 2 large onions, diced
- 2 cups chopped tomatoes
- 1 cup chopped celery
- 1 cup chopped bell pepper
- 4 cloves of garlic, minced
- 1 cup flour
- salt, black pepper, and red pepper flakes
- 3 quarts water or fish stock (recipe in chapter 16)
- bread crumbs to thicken (unless you start with a roux)

Heat the lard in a cast-iron skillet. Add the okra and sauté until tender. Drain. Sauté the onion, celery, bell pepper, and garlic. Put all the vegetables into a large gumbo pot, along with the tomatoes. Sprinkle on some salt, black pepper, and red pepper flakes. Turn the heat up.

While the pot is heating, add enough lard to the skillet to make about 1 cup. Add a cup of flour. Heat and stir, heat and stir, until you have a brown roux. This should take at least 10 minutes, and purists with a strong arm will go for 30 minutes or longer, shooting for a very brown roux.

Stir the roux into the pot. Add the shrimp and perch chunks. Cook for 10 minutes. Serve hot in bowls. The best procedure is to ladle the hot gumbo into bowls and add a dollop of rice in the center. Have plenty of New Orleans French bread ready.

This pot of gumbo will feed 10 or 12 hungry folks. Leftovers are even better.

Bream

Pumpkinseeds, Redbreast, Bluegills, Shellcrackers, Warmouth, Fliers, and a Dozen Other Tasty Fish for Herter's Wolf-Down Hash and Other Recipes

Years ago I was talking to a noted angling editor and fly fisher about doing a book on cooking trout and bass. He thought it was a swell idea, but, he went on, we ought to include "panfish" to broaden the appeal, calling it *Cooking Trout with Culinary Notes on Bass and Other Panfish*. Clearly, he wanted to give trout top billing, but . . . you know me and my big mouth.

"Oh no," I said. "That won't do. Instead, let's call it *Cooking Bass with Culinary Notes on Trout and Other Panfish*."

There followed a long silence. I couldn't see the guy over the telephone at long distance, but I had a feeling that he was quite livid. After that, the book and the author/editor cooled off considerably. I should have learned a lesson from that, but I confess that I still have feelings on the subject of panfish and sunfish. Technically, I suppose, black bass are a member of the sunfish family, but panfish they are not. They grow to 20 pounds or better, far too big to fit into a skillet.

So . . . I have gone against the publishing grain in this book, choosing not to use the terms "panfish" or "sunfish." Instead, I'm treating bass as bass, partly because the largemouth has for some time been the most popular game fish in North America, whether New York likes it or not. Still there are a lot of other "panfish" that have to be included in a book like this, and, for organizational purposes, I have chosen to use the term "bream," a colloquialism sometimes spelled "brim." This is a very common term in many parts of the country, and I think is understood by every American angler to be small hand-shaped fish, such as the bluegill. The cigar-shaped panfish, such as smelt, are covered in other chapters, and the crappie is given its own chapter. Some people call bream "perch," but I find this is too easily confused with the elongated fish such as the yellow perch and the white perch.

Anyhow, there are dozens and dozens of hand-shaped bream in North America, and I include those with big mouths, such as the warmouth and the rock bass. Most of these fish make excellent eating. The big problem is not with catching these fish or cooking them. It's in the eating. Most of us who grew up with bream on the table have no problem, but others don't know how to eat around the bones. The trick is to pull out the top and bottom fins, then hold the fish in the hands and eat it like corn on the cob. This leaves the rib cage and backbone, both of which contain some good pickings. Another method is to lay the fish flat on the plate and pull the meat off the backbone in a strip; turn and strip the other side.

These fish are usually scaled, beheaded, gutted, and cooked whole, but a few people insist on filleting them. This is a lot of work and wastes a lot of good crispy eating, but, shoot, I'll wolf down all you will fillet. Suit yourself. Those who don't like to dress fish should consider my first recipe in which I fry bream whole, guts and all. We'll get to this and a few other recipes later.

Now that I've got your mouth watering, I'll list a few bream ready for the taking. Most people fish for these with worms or crickets, but the expert fly fisher can usually catch more bream, day in and day out, than the bait angler. Most fly-rodders prefer to use

Big Bream on the Grill (p. 108)

top-water cork and balsa bugs, sponge-rubber spiders with rubber legs, and deer-hair floaters. The truth is that wet flies, properly used, are more productive—but many fly-rodders would rather catch one on top than two under the water!

Anyhow, here are a few bream to consider. Many of these are stunted by overpopulation, and some states have very liberal bag limits. Here in Florida where I live, you can keep 50 assorted bream per day per angler, with 100 per angler in possession. So, catch all you want to eat, and have lots of fun doing it. It's a great way to introduce kids to fishing—and to cooking.

Bluegill. This is by far the most popular bream in North America, partly because it is widely stocked in farm ponds, recreational lakes, and so on. Its natural range is from the Great Lakes east to Lake Champlain, south to Florida, and west to Texas. Bluegills are easily taken by live bait, on the fly or surface popper, and with small grubs on tiny jigs fished on light spinning rigs. Most, however, are taken on cane poles or fiberglass "Bream Busters," as the late Lew Childre named the first telescoping fiberglass pole on the American market. Lew considered himself to be God's man for the fishing pole. I used to work for his company, and he considered me his "word man"!

The bluegill can grow rather large—up to 5 pounds—but these are very rare. Doesn't matter, for the smaller ones are better eating. How small? Hand size or smaller. How small? Well . . . don't scoff, but the best ones for eating are three-finger size. Honest. Some people (never mind who) eat them even smaller, frying them up crisp and then crunching them, bones and all.

Pumpkinseed. This colorful fish is the North's answer to the South's bluegill. It ranges from northeastern Canada to Georgia and up the Mississippi River system to Iowa. It will take a wide variety of live baits, flies, and small lures. The pumpkinseed is easily caught from the shore, eliminating the need for a boat, and it is also caught through the ice in winter. It makes purely excellent eating. Don't tell my redneck buddies, but I prefer the pumpkinseed to the bluegill.

Shellcracker, or Red-Ear. This fish runs a little larger than the bluegill and closely resembles the pumpkinseed in appearance. It's a Southern fish, now stocked in California, New Mexico, and elsewhere. Its original range was from southern Illinois, down the Mississippi, south to Florida and Texas. It's a great food fish, but it seldom takes flies, top-water bugs, or light spinning lures. On the other hand, some very large specimens have been caught in Merritt's Mill Pond in Northwest Florida on light jigs fitted with grubs and jig spinners. At one time, this pond was (and maybe still is) an experiment in put-and-take fishing. Believe it or not, only shellcrackers longer than 14 inches could be kept legally! That's a hell of a big bream.

To complicate matters, the shellcracker will form hybrids with bluegill and green sunfish. This usually doesn't matter simply because all bream are good eating and make good sport on light tackle.

Redbreast. The redbreast, found from New Brunswick west to the Alleghenies and south to Florida, makes excellent table fare. A sporting little fish, it takes surface lures, live bait, and small spoons. Interestingly, it is one of the very few bream that can be taken at night.

Flier. This is not as well known as some of the other bream, but it is one of the best targets for the fly fisher. It is almost round in shape, and in coloration it looks like a cross between a shellcracker and a crappie. The flier lives from Virginia to Florida, east to the Mississippi Valley. It might well be the best eating of all the bream, and it readily takes flies as well as live bait.

Spotted Sunfish. Often called stumpknocker, the spotted sunfish lives from South Carolina to Florida and west to Texas. Although its maximum length is less than 6 inches, it's a scrappy little fish and makes good eating. It's thicker than the bluegill, making up a little for its short length. By the way, some people who fish for the large flathead catfish with live hand-size bream will tell you that the stumpknocker makes better bait than the bluegill. (Apparently the flathead is highly selective.) Note also that the warmouth is also called a stumpknocker.

Long-Eared Sunfish. This fish and subspecies live in the St. Lawrence south to Florida and west to Texas. It's a beautiful and tasty little fish, and it will take flies as well as live bait. It feeds mostly on the surface, making it a good target for small balsa and deer hair bugs, and large dry flies.

Green Sunfish. Originally found in the Great Lakes area, the green sunfish moved south into the Mississippi Valley, and west into Colorado. It is generally smaller than the bluegill, but it is popular as tableware in some areas. It loves crickets and will take a fly.

Warmouth. This is a bream with a big mouth. The warmouth can grow to 11 inches long, but the average is about 6 inches. As its name suggests, it will take a variety of live baits and artificial lures. The warmouth is a good table fish, but not a great one.

Rock Bass. Technically a sunfish, not a black bass, the rock bass fits nicely into my "bream" classification. It ranges from Vermont to the Gulf states. It resembles a warmouth but is perhaps a little slimmer. It can grow up to a pound, but the average is closer to half a pound. It is edible, but, like the warmouth, it is not as good as the other bream. It can taste "muddy," and I think it is responsible for the Yankee notion that largemouth bass taste muddy. It's a case of mud on the mind.

Sacramento Perch. This is the only bream west of the Rockies, except stocked shellcrackers and perhaps other introduced species. The largest of the "sunfishes," the Sacramento perch can grow to 10 pounds. It is native to the Sacramento River system, and has been stocked in Nevada and perhaps elsewhere. The fish is usually taken on spinners and live minnows—but, oddly, not on angleworms.

Other Bream. There are dozens of other bream, some of which—such as the beautiful and tasty orange-spotted sunfish—are dismissed as being too small for sport-fishing purposes—but they sure are good on the table, at least to me. There are countless hybrids in some areas, and a few bream are only of regional importance, such as the small Rio Grande perch. In my neck of the woods, we have "hand-painted" bream, sometimes called river bream, that make for good sport on the fly rod and good eating on the table.

In order to beat the bones, some people fillet the fish, but in my opinion this is not the way to go. It makes the eating a little too easy, taking away the ritual of a hunkering down to a fish fry, in which the angler will pile one side of his plate high with bones. Then, when all the fish is gone, everyone can go back and pick the rib cages.

Other people will want to poach or steam the bream for a while, then use the flaked meat in some recipes. It is perhaps the best flaked fish possible! So, be sure to try some patties, or Herter's Wolf-Down Hash described below. Those who prefer small bream, and I count myself in this group, like to fry three-finger bream crisply and eat them bone and all.

Bream are easy to scale, behead, and gut. The heads make a good fish stock. Note also that the small roe sacks are absolutely delicious when fried along with the fish. Some people will tuck the roe sacs inside the body cavity and fry them with the fish, but I like to dust and fry mine separately. In fact, the bream angler will often have enough roe for a mess, owing to the liberal bag limits in some states.

Here are a few suggestions to try.

Bream in the Skillet, with Talking Points

A lot of people I know like to fry bream in a skillet. Let's start first with some talking points.

If you like, you can cut out the rib cages with kitchen shears, as described in a recipe below. Be sure to save these for a gourmet treat, as explained in chapter 15.

If you are cooking a large batch of fish, french fries, and go-withs in a small skillet, you will have a problem keeping it all hot. Some people cook the fish first, then cover them with brown bags, or perhaps put them into brown bags to hold the heat. I do not recommend this practice, since it tends to soften the fish.

How to speed this up is discussed more fully under the catfish fry in chapter 8. In the case of bluegills, I strongly recommend that you cook the fish last, not first. I also recommend that you drain the fish well on brown bags a few at a time. Do not simply pile them atop each other on a platter. If you do, the fish on the bottom will be dripping with grease.

Also be warned that a skillet too full of hot grease can be dangerous, and I have had to deal with more than one fire. It's best to keep a box of baking powder handy. A sprinkle will quickly smother a fire with CO2, thereby depriving it of oxygen. The next best bet is to cover the skillet with a metal lid. Be warned about trying to remove the skillet from the kitchen by hand. This is especially dangerous with cast-iron skillets with hot handles. Trying to carry a skillet across the kitchen can be dangerous enough, and opening the door can cause a rush of air and flame. Whatever you do, do not try to put out the grease fire with water. Some kitchen fire extinguishers may work, but find out before you need it. The best bet is to keep a box of baking soda handy to the stove, always. Fried chicken is just as dangerous as fish.

So, back to the fish fry: Pan-dress the fish, salt inside and out, and dredge in flour or cornmeal. (A batter can also be used, of course, but it is messy and picks up lots of grease.) Heat about an inch of peanut oil (or other good cooking oil) in a skillet. When it is quite hot—almost smoking—put a few fish into the skillet and fry until golden brown on both sides, turning once. Drain the fish on brown bags while you cook another batch. Serve hot with fries and go-withs of your choice.

A.D.'s Butterbeans

Don't tell anybody, but I usually save very small bream to cook for myself or close family members. How small? Two fingers. If they are large enough to take the hook, they are large enough to eat. Some people call these butterbeans.

First scale, gut, and behead the fish. Then make three slashes on either side. Dust them with extra-fine cornmeal and fry in ¼ inch of hot oil in a skillet. Do not deep-fry. It it important that the fish touch the bottom of the skillet, which will produce a brown spot. Fry until quite crispy. Drain and eat whole, bones and all. First, however, you nibble off the crisp ends of the tail and fins.

A.D.'s No-Mess Shore Lunch

Very fresh bream, caught and cooked on the spot, need not be "dressed." Simply knock the scales off them with a spoon, sprinkle with salt, dust with fine meal or flour, and fry in hot grease until nicely browned. The fish can be eaten from around the innards, which will shrink up considerably. This is one of the very best ways to eat small fish, but, admittedly, the method is not for everybody.

Bream in the Deep-Fryer

Dress and dredge the fish as described in previous recipes. Heat at least 4 inches of oil in a deep-fryer to 375 degrees. Fry the fish a few at a time until nicely browned. With a batter, deep-frying works better than skillet-frying, and of course it is faster. Do not remove and drain the fish with a wire strainer or basket strainer. Remove them one at a time with a hand strainer or good tongs. I do not recommend using a fork, which can drop the fish into the hot oil and splatter you good.

Do not put too many fish in the cooker at one time. This will lower the temperature. In fact, it is good to turn up the heat when you add a batch of fish. It is not usually advisable to cook the bream in batches, especially if they are of mixed sizes. Pay attention to each fish, taking it out when done and adding another to take its place. Note that the raw fish will sink. When it floats to the top, it's done, but I like to let mine brown a little longer.

Herter's Wolf-Down Hash

George L. Herter of the old Herter's mail-order house and author of *Bull Cook and Authentic Historical Recipes* didn't have the patience to eat the smaller bream. Instead, he advocated having your wife poach them for a few minutes, then flake off the flesh. Put the flakes into a skillet with a little butter and beef suet. Scramble for a few minutes, then serve hot. The result, Herter says, is a dish that a good man can wolf right down. Indeed it is.

I don't remember Herter's exact recipe, if he had one, but here's what I would recommend.

Note that flaking the fish greatly decreases the bulk. If you feel that you don't have enough to fill everybody up, finely dice some potatoes and brown them along with the onion and fish flakes.

Steam the fish until the flesh flakes easily, but is still toothsome. Set aside. Heat some butter and oil in a skillet and sauté a handful of chopped onion or scallions until browned around the edges. (If you've got scallions, be sure to include about half the green tops.) Add the fish flakes and cook on medium-high heat, stirring gently with a wooden spoon. Serve on plates, flanked with fries, scallions, hush puppies, and so on.

107

Big Bream on the Grill

The larger bluegill and shellcrackers are not very good when fried. At least they are not as good as the small ones. They can have a sort of musky flavor—what's the word?—that I can't describe, but the consensus is that larger bluegills are not good for frying.

Some people who never cook them any other way, and eat only big 'uns, aren't, for the most part, particularly fond of bluegills. Some people beat the perceived "off taste" by filleting the bream, but I can't in good conscience recommend this method because it wastes so much good fish. In any case, I have discovered a way to win them over simply by disguising the fish and cooking them in an unexpected way. They are delicious if properly grilled cooked over charcoal.

The trick is to remove the fins from the fish, top and bottom. But do not use kitchen shears to cut them off, as some food writers tell us to do. If you do, anyone who bites into them will get a mouthful of small, sharp bones or spines. (Note that fish with soft-rayed fins can be trimmed with scissors, but any of the spiny-finned fish must be handled more carefully. Just the other day I was reading a book by a well-known foodie who recommended, in text and illustrations, dressing red snapper in this manner. Don't do it.)

Where were we? Oh yeah. Behead and scale the large bream and make a shallow cut on both sides of the dorsal fin. Carefully pull the fin out and look at it. Each spine that sticks up should have an attached spine underneath. If it isn't attached, it's still in the fish. Also do the bottom fin the same way. Next, use your kitchen shears to cut out the ribs on both sides. (Save the small rib slabs.) You'll now have an elongated fish that does not look like a bream. Call it something else, in case some of your guests will have mud on the mind. (I call mine A.D.'s River-Run Perch.) Now you're ready to cook.

Sprinkle the fish lightly with Tabasco sauce and put them in a nonmetallic container. Stir them about with your hand to coat all sides lightly. Set aside for an hour or so.

When you are ready to grill, sprinkle the fish again with Tabasco and with a little salt. Rig for grilling over charcoal or wood coals. Grease the grill rack and position it 5 or 6 inches over the hot coals. Place the fish on the rack, side by side, and grill for 5 or 6 minutes on both sides.

What to do with the leftover rib cages from the recipe above? See chapter 15 for these and other bonus noshing treats.

Anadromous and Catadromous Fish

Shad, Mullet, Huge Sturgeon, and Tiny Smelts

Anadromous fish live in salt water and ascend freshwater streams to spawn. These include striped bass, salmon, and some of the trout, which have been covered in other chapters. In this chapter, I also include the mullet which, contrary to what other writers have said, spawns in open salt water and moves into brackish and fresh water for most of their lives. Such fish, including the eel (chapter 13), are called catadromous. A few other fish, called amphidromous, are primarily saltwater species but move readily into freshwater to feed or explore. These include the snook, tarpon, and saltwater catfish.

Most of the anadromous fish are noted for their roe, which is taken in spring during the spawning run. These include shad and sturgeon. In contrast, mullet roe is taken in October, when the fish heads for open salt water to spawn.

Shad

Several species of shad can be taken by anglers. The American shad is by far the most important. It's an Atlantic fish that ascends the coastal streams in spring to spawn. That's when anglers go for it

Cooking the American shad is complicated because the fish is quite bony. Some people claim to be able to bone a shad. I won't dispute the claim, but anyone who says it is easy is either a show-off or a damn liar. After the American shad was stocked in some Pacific waters, the California Fish & Game Commission published a booklet with 30-some-odd how-to photos and detailed captions showing, step-to-step, how to get the bones out. Well, by the time I got to step 28, there wasn't enough flesh left to eat.

Some other writers get around this problem by merely specifying "boned fillets" in the recipe! I confess to taking this easy way out. From the book *Food Festival* I learned that the boning technique is demonstrated at the annual Windsor Shad Derby in Windsor, Connecticut, where a shad dinner is also available. Go there.

Anyhow, the American shad on the run ranges from the Gulf of St. Lawrence to the St. Johns River in Florida. Fortunately, the sows are heavy with roe when they start upstream, giving the lucky angler a gourmet treat, if he or she will take advantage of it. Several shad roe recipes are given in chapter 15. Mullet roe, also covered in this chapter, is similar to shad roe and can be cooked by the same methods.

Hickory shad are also taken by sportsmen from Florida to Maine during the spring run. The hickory feeds on smaller fish, making them a good target for the angler using small spinners. The hickories are edible but are not as commonly saved as American shad. Several other smaller species of shad live in our streams, lakes, and especially in large man-made impoundments. These are not often eaten by anglers—but, I can tell you, the roe and white roe are very, very good.

In any case, here are some shad recipes to try.

Smoked Mullet and Avocado (p. 116)

Long-Baked Shad

The shad is an oily fish that holds up well to this method of cooking. The long, slow baking at moderate temperature will soften the bones. It's best to scale the shad and cook it whole.

The French cook a European shad by the slow-baking method to deal with the bones. The fish is basted from time to time with melted butter and apple cider. I like it. Try this recipe by the French method—using good hard cider, if you've got it.

- shad
- bacon
- vinegar
- salt

Preheat the oven to 250 degrees. Using a strip of the bacon, grease a heavy roasting pan. (I use an oblong fish fryer with a lid.) Tuck a strip or two of bacon inside the shad and place it into the pan. Almost cover the fish with lightly salted water, then add a strip or two of bacon on top. Add 1 tablespoon vinegar. Bring to a boil on the stove-top.

Cover the pan and carefully put it into the center of the oven. Bake for 5 hours (depending on the size of the fish—the rule of thumb is to cook it for an hour and a half per pound), adding a little water from time to time if needed. Toward the end of the calculated cooking time, pour off any remaining water. Leave the top off the pan and bake for 30 minutes. Turn on the broiler and cook until the bacon is browned. Serve with boiled new potatoes and a hearty green salad.

Shad with Top Milk

This rich, old recipe goes back to the days when cow's milk was used unhomogenized, in which case the cream rose to the top of the jar. Hence, it was called top milk. These days, cream from the supermarket will have to do, unless you or your neighbor own a good cow. This is a rich, filling dish, partly because of the oily shad and partly because of the butter and cream. Scrumptious, but fattening.

- 2 pounds boned shad fillets
- 1 cup top milk or heavy cream, warmed
- ¼ cup melted butter
- salt and black pepper to taste

Preheat the oven to 400 degrees. Place the fish in a greased baking dish of suitable size. Sprinkle with salt and pepper and drizzle with melted butter. Bake in the center of the oven for 20 minutes. Add the cream and bake for another 20 minutes, basting a time or two with the pan juice. Serve hot along with new potatoes, greens, and so on, with some good bread.

Planked Shad

Baking shad fillets are an old favorite in Connecticut, dating back to Colonial days.

To proceed, preheat the oven to 400 degrees. Grease an oak plank large enough to hold the fish and small enough to fit into the oven. Lay the fillets skin-side down. Brush with melted butter and bake in the center of the oven for 20 minutes. Brush again with butter and lay a border of fried apple slices. Bake for another 20 minutes. Serve on the plank, garnished with parsley. I'll take a little of that apple cider with my serving.

Note: For more on plank cookery, see the Planked Salmon recipe in chapter 3, using mashed potatoes instead of fried apples.

Shad Neapolitan

Tomatoes go well with this Italian-style stewed fish, featuring also garlic and olive oil. Note that there is a difference between a fish stew and stewed fish.

- 1 to 2 pounds shad fillets, boned
- 4 medium tomatoes, diced (1-inch pieces)
- ½ cup tomato or V-8 juice
- 1 medium to large onion, chopped
- 1 green bell pepper, chopped
- 5 garlic cloves, crushed
- ¼ cup vermouth
- 2 tablespoons parsley, finely chopped
- 2 tablespoon olive oil
- sea salt and freshly ground black pepper
- 1 teaspoon fresh basil, minced

Heat the olive oil in a large skillet. (An electric skillet will be great.) Sauté the onions, garlic, and bell pepper until tender. Add the tomatoes, tomato juice, parsley, salt, pepper, and basil. Simmer for 10 minutes, carefully stirring once or twice with a wooden spoon. Add the fillets and simmer for 10 minutes, or until the fillets flake easily when tested with a fork. Plate the fillets, topping with the tomato mixture. Have ready plenty of chewy Italian bread and table wine.

Mullet

Several species of mullet live in the estuaries along the lower Atlantic and Gulf Coasts. (Other species grow in the Mediterranean, and these were actually farmed by the ancient Romans and the Egyptians.) The reputation of the mullet is hard to figure. It is highly prized in parts of the Florida Panhandle, and is a popular breakfast dish in Pensacola. Yet, in New Orleans, less than 200 miles away, it is considered a trash fish! Personally, I like its rich, nutty flavor. It is also highly nutritious.

At one time, anglers thought the mullet could not be taken by hook and line, but these days they are taken on tiny salmon egg hooks baited with okra seeds or some such vegetation. They can also be taken on tiny flies, especially when they are feeding on the surface scum. The fly should, of course, look like a blob of vegetable matter. Most anglers who tie their flies can simply use their dry-fly rejects. The cast-net, however, is much more productive if you know how to throw one. Once you spot a school of mullet nosing the surface, it's easy to catch a mess or two. They should be dressed quickly and used very fresh.

In Florida, many culinary sports will cook the "gizzard" along with the mullet. It is simply an organ that grinds the fish's food, usually vegetable matter. (Before cooking, it is split, turned, and cleaned.) But don't get too excited. The gizzard is tough and tasteless, although it is a pretty white muscle. The real gourmet fare is the roe—and the white roe. Dried mullet roe was highly prized by the Egyptian pharaohs and it is still popular in the Mediterranean and Japan. It sells at very high prices. For more on this delicacy and on fish roe in general, see chapter 15. Also, a few recipes for mullet roe and shad roe (which is similar) are included in this chapter.

Here are some suggestions to try.

Baked Mullet

This is an old Middle Eastern recipe for the Mediterranean red mullet, using parchment. I find that aluminum foil and American gray or white mullet also work. Use whole fish about 13 inches long, allowing 1 fish per person. The olive oil seems to work wonders on our mullet!

- 6 freshly caught mullet
- 1 cup olive oil
- juice and zest of 2 lemons
- 1 cup dry fresh parsley, finely chopped
- salt and black pepper to taste
- 1 teaspoon thyme
- ½ teaspoon paprika

Preheat the oven to 350 degrees. In a bowl, coat the fish inside and out with olive oil. Place each fish on a separate piece of aluminum foil and brush with olive oil. Use all the olive oil. Wrap each fish and seal with a double fold. Place the packets on a baking sheet in the center of the oven. Cook for 35 minutes.

Turn off the oven and let the fish coast for a few minutes. Then unwrap the fish and transfer to a heated serving platter, or place on individual plates. Mix the rest of the ingredients and sprinkle evenly over the fish. Serve with rice and a colorful salad.

Grilled Mullet

Although this is an Italian recipe for the Mediterranean red mullet, adapted here from *The Sicilian Gentleman's Cookbook* (a delightful work), it works nicely for American mullet. I cook it from Florida mullet—and Florida citrus.

In Sicily, I understand, small red mullet are grilled and eaten whole, innards and all, and in France red mullet is sometimes called the Woodcock of the Sea. The connection? Woodcock are also eaten whole, trail and all, sometimes after aging for several days or longer. Remember also that the mullet has an edible gizzard—and therefore must be a bird.

3 mullet
¼ cup extra-virgin olive oil
¼ cup fish stock (recipe in chapter 16)
¼ cup dry white wine
¼ cup butter
juice of 1 lemon and 1 orange
grated zest of 1 lemon and 1 orange
Tabasco or other hot sauce (optional)
salt and freshly ground black pepper to taste

Scale, draw, and fillet the mullet. Stir some salt and pepper into the olive oil and put it into a shallow dish. Flip-flop the fillets in it and set aside for an hour, turning from time to time. Build a fire in your grill so that the coals will be ready. While waiting, heat the fish stock, wine, lemon zest, and orange zest in a saucepan. Turn off the heat and add the lemon juice, orange juice, and butter, along with a little Tabasco sauce, if wanted. Keep warm.

When the coals are ready, grease the rack and grill the fillets about 3 inches above the heat for about 4 minutes on each side, turning once, or until the fish flakes easily when tested with a fork. Serve hot, topped with the sauce. Servings? I'll require at least 2 fillets. White rice and black beans go nicely with this dish, along with a citrus salad or grilled pineapple and bread.

This dish can also be prepared under an oven broiler, with the fish about 3 inches from the heat. I finish mine off skin-side down, letting the soft side brown nicely.

Sopchoppy Mullet Tails

I ran across this while browsing the menu, written on a blackboard, at Ma's Restaurant in Sopchoppy, Florida, a few years ago. Turned out that the "tails" were simply fillets (without the tail fins).

mullet fillets
white cornmeal, finely ground
cooking oil for deep-frying
salt and pepper

Salt and pepper the fillets, shake in a bag with the meal, and fry in hot oil (375 degrees) until nicely browned. Drain and serve with fried okra, hush puppies, grits, and fried onion rings, along with a goblet of sweet ice tea.

Mullet Fillets with Lime Sauce

Mullet, a fatty fish, goes nicely when baked and served with a lime sauce. Here's what you'll need.

- 2 pounds mullet fillets
- ½ cup melted butter
- juice and grated zest of 1 lime
- 1 medium onion, grated
- salt and pepper to taste

Preheat the oven to 350 degrees. While waiting, mix the butter, lime juice and zest, onion, salt, and pepper. Wrap the fillets loosely in aluminum foil, place in the center of the oven, and bake for 30 minutes. Open the foil and broil for 3 or 4 minutes. Plate the fillets and top with some of the lime sauce. Serve with swamp salad (heart of palm), sliced tomatoes, and Cuban bread.

Old-Time Salt Mullet Breakfast

At one time, salt mullet was a staple in rural Florida and up into Alabama and Georgia. Every grocery store sold them from wooden boxes, and the old rolling stores carried them into the countryside before automobiles were common. They were often eaten for breakfast, a tradition that still hangs on in some areas.

Always, the salt mullet were sold butterflied, with the scales on. Before cooking, they were soaked in water for several hours, or overnight. Then they were dusted with cornmeal and fried in a skillet.

The menu included grits (with butter), fried eggs, biscuits, and hot coffee, with plenty of good sugar cane syrup to serve over biscuit halves at the end of the meal. After eating such a breakfast at sunup, a good man could plow all day with only a light lunch.

My father, a peanut farmer, was fond of this breakfast, and I have eaten it many times. Finding it a little heavy, my family also like several slices of vine-ripened tomato on the side.

(Note: It's easy to salt your own mullet. Since the mullet has limited distribution, however, I have described the technique in the Crapple chapter.) Of course, salt cod and other salt fish, are sometimes available sealed in plastic in supermarkets instead of wooden boxes.

Outer Banks Mullet

The mullet is enjoyed along the Outer Banks of North Carolina, where it is often served with cold watermelon slices. Be sure to try this with mullet, shad, or any other good fatty fish. It's best to scale and fillet the mullet, leaving the skin on.

- 2 pounds mullet fillets
- bacon drippings
- sea salt and black pepper
- cold watermelon, sliced

Sprinkle the fillets with salt and refrigerate for an hour or longer. Preheat the broiler and position the rack about 4 inches from the heat source. Fit the fillets skin-side down in a well-greased shallow broiling pan. (Do not use the rack.) Brush with bacon drippings. Sprinkle with pepper. Broil for 8 to 10 minutes, or until the meat flakes easily when tested with a fork. Serve with slices of cold watermelon.

Sturgeon Salad

This interesting and attractive dish comes from Eastern Europe, adapted here from *The Best of Ukrainian Cuisine*. It works nicely with American sturgeon and red salmon roe.

- 1 ½ pounds thick sturgeon fillet
- 1 medium onion, chopped
- 8 hard-boiled chicken eggs
- 2 tins small sardines in oil
- ¼ pound butter
- ¼ pound red caviar
- salt
- lettuce leaves
- fresh parsley sprigs

Simmer the sturgeon in water with a chopped onion on very low heat for 15 or 20 minutes. Drain and chill the fillet, then carefully cut it into 1-inch slices. Arrange the slices in the middle of a serving platter, leaving some space at the top. Arrange the sardines around the sturgeon.

Cut the boiled eggs in half, putting the yolks aside. Stuff the egg whites with red caviar and arrange around the edge of the platter. Garnish with parsley and serve on lettuce leaves, along with dark bread and vodka.

Azerbaijani Kabobs

This popular dish is great for cooking over charcoal. I, for one, appreciate the facts that no lengthy marinade is required and that the spit isn't crowded with vegetable chunks, leaving lots of room for fish. The vegetables are served raw on the side.

- 2 pounds sturgeon fillet
- 2 medium tomatoes
- 12 scallions
- ¼ cup minced parsley
- ¼ cup sour cream
- ¼ cup fresh lemon juice
- 2 tablespoons melted butter
- sea salt to taste
- lemon wedges (garnish)

Rig for grilling over charcoal. Cut the fish into 1 ½-inch cubes and sprinkle with salt. In a bowl, mix the sour cream and lemon juice. Toss the fish in the mixture, coating all sides. Skewer the fish chunks and grill 4 inches above the coals for 12 minutes, turning and basting with melted butter every few minutes, or until the fish are tender and brindled around the outside. Serve hot on a bed of rice, with tomato slices and chilled green onions on the side, along with lemon wedges. I like the scallions served in a small glass of ice.

Smelts

Most of the world's smelts are anadromous. These include the eulachon of Alaska and the rainbow smelt, often caught in brackish water in New England. Two species, the grunion and the capelin, spawn in the surf and can be taken in large numbers in season. Fortunately for inland anglers, a lot of smelts live in lakes. These are taken by ice fishermen and upstream during the spring spawning run. Several other species can be taken in fresh water at one time or another.

To dress smelt, try cutting the head off with kitchen shears and then running your finger along the bottom to force out the innards. This will speed things up considerably when you have a large batch to clean and aren't too particular—or fry them whole, as detailed in the first recipe below.

All of the smelts are excellent eating, but they spoil easily and should be iced soon after capture. One of the famous smelts, the Alaskan eulachon or hooligan, contains so much oil that the Indians inserted a wick in it and burned it like a candle. (It is often called candlefish.) Its oil is also highly prized for cooking and as a condiment, rather like olive oil. The rest of the smelts available in American waters are pretty much unsung, except in local spots where the spring run can be exciting.

Here are a few recipes to try. Also remember that the fish's oil content makes them great for grilling or broiling. Most folks fry them, however, in which case the oil can be a bit much for some tastes. If they are deep-fried and dumped to drain in a pile, the ones on bottom are likely to be dripping with oil. Proper draining will help, or, better, spread them out on a brown bag and keep them hot in a slow oven until the whole batch has been fried.

Hooligan Fry

A lot of squeamish people will want to behead and gut smelt before cooking. Culinary sports, however, may want to eat like some of the natives. The fish are cooked whole, ungutted. (Note: This method led to my favorite way of cooking small bluegills, horneyheads, and such.)

very fresh smelt
flour
finely ground cornmeal
salt
salt water
cooking oil

Build a good fire and have some coals ready. Mix some cornmeal and flour, about half and half, and add a little salt. Wash the smelt in salt water and dust with the cornmeal. Heat about an inch of oil in a skillet. Fry the smelt a few at a time until nicely browned and crisp all around.

Serve hot. The flesh can be stripped off the backbone with the fingers, which leaves the innards untouched in the rib cage, or, if they are crisply fried, you can eat them whole, bones, innards, and all.

Buffalo Burgers with Fire-Roasted Pepper (p. 125)

Trash or Treasure?

Spotted Suckers for Jimmy Carter, Horneyheads for Me, and "Whatyagot?" for You

Here are a few culinary treasures from the proverbial trash pile, with a few recipes and crucial preparation notes.

Suckers

In his book *An Outdoor Journal*, President Jimmy Carter spoke fondly of the spotted sucker for sport and food. It lives from Minnesota to Pennsylvania, south to Florida and Texas, and is remembered fondly by those with Georgia on the mind. The white sucker, which grows from Canada to Florida and west to Montana, is larger than the spotted sucker (weighing up to 8 pounds), but as table fare it is not quite as desirable. Both fish are quite bony and are often ground in a sausage mill to make fish patties.

The popular spotted and white suckers have a rather large range, but others are quite local. The humpback sucker, which also makes good eating, lives only in the lower Colorado River basin. It grows to 10 pounds and can be taken on hook and line. The longnose sucker grows across North America from Alaska to Maine, but only in cold waters. There are several others, and the picture is complicated by fish of the same family, especially the buffalo, which I have covered under a separate heading.

The northern redhorse is a colorful fish extending roughly from upper Arkansas to Eastern Canada. It's good eating—and can weigh up to 12 pounds. The silver redhorse lives from Manitoba to the St. Lawrence and south to Missouri and Alabama. It is generally smaller than the northern redhorse, but it is good table fare.

There are other suckers, and they can be identified by the familiar down-turned sucker-mouth. As far as I know, all the suckers are edible, but some are better than others, or worse than others, depending on your mind-set. The northern hog sucker, for example, available from Minnesota to the Gulf of Mexico, is not highly regarded because of its soft flesh.

There are several species of carpsuckers, such as the quillback, and all are edible and are sometimes sold commercially, I understand, as carp. They live mostly in the Mississippi and Ohio River systems, but they are also found in New England and the Southeastern Gulf states.

A lot of the suckers are quite plentiful in their range and are taken in large numbers during the spring spawning run with fish gigs, traps, or gill nets. Sucker fishing is specially popular in Missouri, where an annual sucker fry is held each spring.

In winter, the suckers are baited with cottonseed cake or some such vegetable matter. Once the "sucker hole" has been established, the fish are caught on hook and line using a dough ball bait of some sort. Such baits are widely available commercially, but the complete sucker angler will have his own secret recipe.

When fishing for suckers, usually on tight line, it's hard to tell when you get a bite—but when you stick a hook into one you've got a real fight on your hands. I think they pull better than most other fish. They are also tasty, if properly prepared. Here are some suggestions.

Freshwater Drum

This fish, which grows up to 60 pounds, is the freshwater cousin of several saltwater drums. Sometimes called sheepshead, gaspergou, gou, or goo, and half a dozen other names, they live in the large lakes and streams of mid-America, south into Tennessee and Alabama. Although they are sold commercially (maybe under other names), their flesh is not all that good. It does not keep well, and your catch should be gutted and put on ice as soon as possible after capture.

One night long ago, I once caught a huge drum on a large crawfish (the drum's favorite food) while after catfish on the Tennessee River. The thing must have weighed 40 pounds, and it was almost dead by the time I finally got it into the boat. It was summer and I fished all night. After daylight, I put the fish in the trunk of the car, along with a couple of catfish, and drove some 50 miles to my home. By then the the fish was ripe, I tell you, with the eyes bulging out, and was none too tasty. (The catfish were fine.) If I had done my homework, the big fish would have provided lots of good eating. I don't recommend it for frying, grilling, baking, or broiling—but there are other opinions on the matter, and I've seen recipes for fried and broiled fillets. Still, I think the fish is best when poached and used in casserole-type dishes.

Here are a few recipes to try.

Drum-and-Rice Creole Casserole

I like to make this dish with freshwater drum, grass carp, and such fish as largemouth bass as well as saltwater drum. The recipe smacks of New Orleans Creole cookery, in which the drum is called "gou."

- 1 pound drum fillets
- ½ cup chopped bacon
- 1 cup long-grained white rice
- 2 cups chopped fresh tomatoes
- 1 cup chopped onion
- 1 cup chopped celery with green tops
- ½ cup chopped red bell pepper
- ½ cup chopped green bell pepper
- 3 or 4 cloves garlic, minced or crushed
- 1 cup fish stock (recipe in chapter 16) or chicken broth
- salt, black pepper, and cayenne to taste

Skin the fillets and cut them into 1-inch chunks. Using a little bacon fat, grease a 2-quart casserole dish and set aside. Preheat the oven to 350 degrees.

Fry the bacon until crisp in a large cast-iron skillet. Add the onion, bell peppers, and garlic. Sauté until the onion is tender. Put the skillet contents into a large bowl and mix in the other stuff. Turn out into the casserole dish. Bake for 45 minutes to an hour, until the rice is tender. Serve for lunch (or dinner) with a good bread and a large salad.

Drum Chow Mein

For this idea I am in debt to the *Lake Erie Cookbook,* published by the Ohio Sea Grant College Program at Ohio State University. Here's my version, with a little more soy.

- 2 cups cooked drum flakes
- 2 cups cooked rice
- 1 can cream of mushroom soup
- 1 can chow mein noodles (3-ounce size)
- 1 cup diced celery with green tops
- ½ cup diced onion
- ½ cup freeze-dried cashew nuts
- 1 tablespoon soy sauce
- freshly ground black pepper to taste

Preheat the oven to 350 degrees and grease a 1 ½-quart casserole dish suitable for serving. In a large bowl mix the soup, 1 cup chow mein noodles, and the rest of the ingredients with your hands. Turn out into the casserole. Smooth out and scatter the remaining noodles on top. Bake in the center of the oven for 20 minutes. Turn the heat off and let it coast for 5 minutes or so, while you set the table. Eat hot with some San Francisco sourdough bread and a vegetable or two.

Drum Pie

Here's a neat way to cook a drum. You'll need 1 pound of poached fish, flaked. A 2-pound drum will be about right. If you've got a larger drum, freeze the rest of the cooked flakes and save for another pie or another recipe. Or make several pies at once.

- 1 pound flaked precooked drum
- 2 medium potatoes, diced
- 1 medium onion, diced
- ½ cup chopped scallions with part of green tops
- ½ cup cream
- ¼ cup butter (divided)
- 3 tablespoons flour
- single pastry for 9-inch pie
- salt and black pepper to taste

Preheat the oven to 400 degrees. Melt about half the butter in a skillet. Sauté the onion, scallions, and potatoes until tender. (Do not brown.)

In a saucepan, melt the rest of the butter. Add the flour. Cook and stir with a wooden spoon until smooth. Add the cream slowly, stirring as you go. Mix in the onion and potato mix from the skillet, along with some salt and pepper. Using your hands, mix in the flaked fish.

Turn the mixture out into a greased 9-inch pie pan. Place the pastry on top. Punch in a few holes with a fork and flute the edges by pinching with your fingers. Put into the center of the oven and bake for 20 minutes. Serve hot, along with green peas, mashed potatoes, salad, and chewy bread for a light meal.

Eel Teriyaki

Here's one of my favorite ways to cook eel fillets on a charcoal grill or over hot coals from a campfire. Note that the whole eel can be grilled, but the backbone complicates the cooking and the eating. The Japanese, by the way, dearly love eel and grill it at festive occasions.

- 2 or 4 eel fillets, cut into 4-inch lengths
- ½ cup good soy sauce
- ½ cup sake or dry vermouth
- 1 tablespoon dark brown sugar
- 1 tablespoon bacon drippings
- ½ tablespoon Asian sesame oil
- ½ tablespoon grated ginger root
- juice and grated zest of 1 lemon
- 2 cloves garlic, crushed

Mix all the ingredients, adding the eel pieces last. Marinate for an hour or longer. Strain out the eel and drain. Heat the marinade to a light boil in a pan and save it for basting.

Rig for grilling, placing the rack about 4 inches over the hot coals or heat source. Grill for 5 minutes on each side, basting several times. Pile the eel off to the side of the grill and let it coast a while. Serve hot with rice, steamed vegetables, and sake.

Note: If you are using whole eel, cook it longer and cut down to the bone to make sure it is done.

The Other Cats

Most of the freshwater catfish of North America make very good eating and have been covered in a separate chapter. Two saltwater catfish, both of which can be taken in brackish water and in streams near salt water, are almost always cussed and thrown away—but these are really good eating and and are discussed in more length in Chapter 12.

Also, two exotic catfish (the walking cat and the armored cat) are on the loose in Florida. These are covered in the next chapter.

Bowfin

This is beyond a doubt the meanest fish in North America and will fight with no holds barred. Because you get it in a net doesn't mean you've got him, as he has been known to twist his way through the bottom and plop back into the water. I know one big burly bass angler who is actually afraid of them, and will shoot them with a pistol before trying to get a hook out of their mouths. Fortunately for fly-rodders, they are not interested in gnats and prefer a large spoon dressed with a pork rind.

These brawlers, which can weigh 20 pounds or better, are also known as grindle, grinnel, dogfish, cypress trout, mud fish, and dogfish. These primitive fish range up and down the Mississippi system and spread east to Florida and West to Texas. Florida and Louisiana are hot spots.

The fish is edible, but not choice. It is best when cooked right away. If it is kept very long, the flesh becomes rather mushy, like cotton. The best bet is to skin the thing right away, fillet it, and fry it fast in a hot skillet.

In Louisiana, believe it or not, the roe of bowfin is made into Cajun Caviar and sold commercially. I caught a big sow grinnel a few years ago beside a cypress tree that grew in the shallow water near my dock on Dead Lakes (in Florida). The thing must have weighed 16 or 17 pounds. I dressed it out and was surprised to find over a pound of roe in it. The egglets were about the size of BBs, and were black on one side and yellow on the other!

A.D.'s Cypress Trout Stir-Fry

The last time I ate a bowfin was when I had a bumper crop of big red tomatoes in my container garden on the dock. As soon as I got the thing out of the water, I filleted it and, in short, had a Vietnamese stir-fry dish going within minutes. It was delicious, and I saved the head to fertilize my tomatoes.

1 pound bowfin fillets
4 tomatoes, chopped
1 onion, chopped
¼ cup peanut oil
¼ cup fish sauce
more fish sauce to taste
1 tablespoon flour
½ tablespoon white vinegar
½ tablespoon brown sugar
black pepper (no salt)

Cut the fillets into chunks. Mix a little water into the flour to make a paste; set aside ready to go. Have all the other ingredients at hand.

Heat 1 tablespoon of the oil in a skillet or wok. Brown the fish a few pieces at a time and drain. Add more oil as needed. When all the fish have been browned, sprinkle with fish sauce and black pepper. (No salt will be needed if you use the fish sauce generously.)

Add a little more oil to the wok if needed and brown the onions. Add the tomatoes, another 2 tablespoons of oil, about a half a cup of water, and the brown sugar, stirring with a wooden spoon as you go. Simmer on low heat for a few minutes, until the tomatoes are soft. Add the fish and the flour paste. Stir with a wooden spoon until a nice sauce develops. Add more fish sauce to taste and stir in the vinegar. Serve hot with rice. Have more fish sauce on the table along with a pepper mill.

Gar Balls Toogoodoo

This recipe has been adapted from *The South Carolina Wildlife Cookbook,* to which it was submitted by James M. Bishop, a culinary sport from Charleston.

2 pounds flaked gar
1 pound cooked potatoes, mashed
2 large onions, minced
1 cup mixed chopped parsley, green onion tops, or celery tops
½ cup prepared mustard sauce
½ cup vinegar
flour
salt and pepper to taste
cooking oil

Mix the mustard and vinegar in a bowl. Stir in the gar meat, potatoes, onions, and greens. Using your hands, shape the mixture into 1½-inch balls. Carefully roll these in the mustard sauce and then in flour. Set aside while you heat 1 inch of oil in a cast-iron skillet. Fry the balls a few at a time and drain on brown bags. Serve hot.

A.D.'s Gar Backstrap Medallions

When dressing the gar, I cut and remove the two backstraps (which are shaped somewhat like pork tenderloins), and I cut them into slices about ½ inch thick. The thickness is very important. If they are too thick, the gristle in the flesh may be objectionable, but when thin enough, and crisply fried, it won't be noticed.

Simply salt the medallions, shake in a bag with flour, and deep-fry until well-browned and crisp. Serve as you would any other fried fish.

Carp

Cy Littlebee, a rather folksy culinary sport of Missouri, who put together a book on cooking fish and game, said it best: "I reckon carp has been a favorite fish for more centuries than you or I'd care to live. It ain't rated top very often in Missouri, but in Europe and Asia, they sat a heap of store by carp as far back as history goes."

Cy was right, not only because the carp can make good table fare but also because it is popular as a sport fish. Fishing carp in England and some other parts of Europe is something of a cult, requiring special ultralight stealth equipment. In short, the carp has been called the wariest fish in the world. So . . . the American angler has been missing out on lots of good fishing challenge—and some eating.

A native of Asia, the carp was brought to Europe early as early as 350 B.C., when described by Aristotle. It was introduced to North America in 1886 by the United States Fish Commission as a food and sport fish. But the expected demand for the carp didn't grow as fast as the fish, and it has been multiplying ever since. My guess is that more are taken these days by "bow fishing" than by rod and reel. A few carp are taken on the fly, but serious anglers go after them with the classic dough bait, and anglers disagree strongly over the ingredients and exact measures (or proportions) used in the stuff. The late A.J. McClane, the fishery guru of *Field & Stream* magazine, has said that a treatise on carp fishing reads like a cookbook.

(The grass carp or white amur isn't really a carp and has been treated in the next chapter as an exotic fish since it has only recently been introduced in North American waters.)

In any case, the carp grows up to 80 pounds or so, and a 55-pounder has been recorded at Clearwater Lake in Minnesota. Ten-pounders are common and are said to be cruising our large lakes and impoundments like atomic submarines. The larger ones may be more desirable for cooking purposes simply because the bones are easier to remove in the larger fish.

Most people immediately get mud on the mind whenever carp is mentioned. Some expert carp lovers recommend that the fish be skinned and that the dark meat along the lateral line be removed. The bones? The European cooks and cookbooks seem to ignore this problem, but a lot of people in America simply grind the meat in a sausage mill.

Here are a few recipes to try. See also the carp rib appetizer in chapter 15.

Istanbul Carp

Cut some 1-inch steaks from a rather large carp. In Istanbul, according to *A Turkish Cookbook,* to eat this dish means you have good taste. Well, at least the Turks know that red wine is better than white!

6 center-cut carp steaks
½ cup fish stock (recipe in chapter 16)
½ cup vinegar
½ cup good red wine
1 large onion, finely chopped
¼ cup sultanas (white raisins)
¼ cup walnuts, finely chopped
juice of 1 lemon
lemon slices (for garnish)
2 tablespoons parsley, finely chopped (for garnish)
salt and freshly ground black pepper

Place the fish steaks in a shallow dish. Sprinkle with salt and chopped onion. Pour in the vinegar. Marinate in a cool place for 2 hours. When you are ready to resume, place the fish in a suitable pan and add the stock. Bring to heat and simmer for 12 minutes, or until the fish flakes easily when tested with a fork. Remove the fish to a heated serving platter.

Add the rest of the ingredients, except for the garnishes, to the pan and simmer until reduced by about a third, stirring as you go with a wooden spoon. Pour the sauce over the carp steaks. Sprinkle with parsley and serve with a lemon slice on the side. This dish goes nicely with a pilaf.

Carp St. Nickolas

According to Atanas Slavov's *Traditional Bulgarian Cooking,* this is a traditional dish eaten on St. Nickolas day in the Eastern Orthodox church, in which St. Nickolas is believed to be the guardian of fishermen and their catch.

7-pound carp
1 red onion, finely chopped
1 white onion, finely chopped
1 cup white wine
¾ cup crushed walnuts
¼ cup bread crumbs
6 tablespoons olive oil (divided)
2 tablespoons tomato paste
2 tablespoons flour
10 peppercorns, finely crushed
3 allspice berries, finely crushed
2 bay leaves
salt and pepper to taste

Scale and gut the carp. Preheat the oven to 350 degrees. Sprinkle the carp inside and out with salt and black pepper. In a skillet or saucepan, heat 2 tablespoons of the olive oil, red onion, walnuts, bread crumbs, and 1 tablespoon water. Stuff the carp with this mixture and close with skewers or sew with twine. Place the stuffed carp in a greased baking pan. Pour ½ cup boiling water over the carp and bake in the center of the oven for an hour.

While waiting, put the rest of the olive oil in a saucepan, along with 3 tablespoons water and white onion. Simmer for a few minutes, then stir in the tomato paste. Mix the flour in 2 tablespoons of water, then stir it into the sauce, along with the black pepper, allspice, wine, and bay leaves. Simmer until you have a nice sauce. Pour over the carp and bake for another 2 or 3 minutes. Feeds six.

Baked Carp Patties

Most fish patties are fried, but they can be baked as well. Here's an easy recipe to try.

- 2 cups ground carp flesh
- 2 cups Cornbread Stuffing (recipe in chapter 16)
- salt and pepper to taste
- 1 tablespoon fish sauce or soy sauce

Preheat the oven to 350 degrees and grease a baking sheet. Mix all the ingredients and shape into patties about ¾ inch thick. Place the patties on the baking sheet and cook in the center of the oven for 15 minutes. Serve hot. I like a little ketchup with mine, but hollandaise will do.

Also, try this cooked as a cake. Simply put all the mixture into a greased baking dish suitable for serving. Bake for 20 minutes. Serve up with a large spoon, or cut into squares.

Squawfish or Pikeminnow

Believe it or not, these large fish, weighing up to 80 pounds, are technically a minnow! They can be taken in California, Washington, and Oregon on natural bait and artificial lures. Squawfish are edible, but bony. Smoking is perhaps the best way to prepare them.

Chubs, Horneyheads, and Stonerollers

Someone has written that a cooked chub resembles a wad of cotton stuffed with needles, referring, of course, to its soft flesh and many bones. The chub in question, however, was probably a species from Europe, where a chub grows up to 10 pounds and provides some angling value. Several smaller species thrive in North America and a number of other species are called chubs, including the fallfish, a minnow of eastern North America, which Thoreau said tastes like "brown paper salted."

When I was a kid, my family often held fish fries under bridges over the upper Choctawhatchee River. We kept and fried just about everything we caught, including something we called a "roach." My guess is that it was a creek chub, but I'm not sure. In any case, they were not bad eating if cooked very fresh and crisply fried.

We also ate a small fish called a "horneyhead," which was, as best I can tell, technically a stoneroller. These are very tasty, and, in fact, they are highly regarded in parts of Tennessee, where they are taken in small streams on wet flies and a tiny spinner.

So . . . it's fun to take the kids fishing and to cook whatever they catch!

Don't worry. None of the freshwater fish in North America are are poisonous. Gar roe, however, can be toxic to man, and, of course, some of the puffers and other saltwater fish may be suspect.

Laotian Soup

Although the snakehead can be cooked any way you want it, many American anglers might prefer to start with a milder presentation, which was once served in the Royal Palace at Luang Prabang, according to Phia Sing's *Traditional Recipes of Laos*. If the snakehead doesn't yet prowl your favorite fishing hole, you might want to try the soup with any good fish with firm white flesh.

1 snakehead about 2 feet long
1 stalk lemongrass, finely chopped
several garlic cloves, minced
5 scallions, chopped
1 tablespoon rice
coriander leaves (cilantro)
fish sauce to taste
salt and pepper to taste
water

Fillet the snakehead and cut it into 1-inch chunks. Put about 2 cups water into a pot and bring to a boil. Add the fish and rice. Simmer for 10 minutes. Add the chopped onion, garlic, lemongrass, and fish sauce. Cook for 10 or 15 minutes. Taste, add a little salt if needed (depending on how much fish sauce you used), and ladle into serving bowls. Sprinkle with minced coriander leaves and add some freshly ground black pepper. Serve hot and have a few lemon wedges for those who want more lemon flavor.

Asian Swamp Eels

This interesting creature will sometimes stick its head high out of the water and look at you for what seems a long time. It actually sticks its sail into the bottom to help support the head lift, and does so to breathe air or probably more often just for the hell of it. This makes the fish almost impossible to eradicate with chemicals once it has become established in a body of water. And swamp eels are now in Florida and slowly heading north, as the creature can also cross over land. Moreover, it can live for a long time without eating.

A fierce predator, its diet consists of frogs, crawfish, worms, and small fish. Hence, the swamp eel is often caught with live bait.

Anyhow, the swamp eel is considered a delicacy in Southeast Asia, and it is especially useful as a market fish because it can live out of the water for a long time. If you catch one, put it into a wet burlap bag and save it live until you are ready to feast on it.

Recipes? I would especially recommend the Eel Teriyaki recipe in chapter 13. Also, in Burma the swamp eel is used to make a fish-bladder soup (for more on using swim bladders and other innards, see chapter 15 and the recipe for Fish Head and Oyster Soup).

Armored Catfish

These things from South and Central America were introduced into Florida several years ago. As the name implies, they have bony plates that cover the body like large scales. They are caught on live bait and can grow quite large. The flesh is edible—if you can get at it. In the Amazon basin, the natives toss the fish into a fire to crack the shell. Then they are raked out and shucked. Try it if you catch one.

Walking Catfish

These immigrants from Asia also grow, in one species or another, in Africa. The thing made believe-it-or-not news about 40 years ago when it was first seen walking across roads in Florida. Apparently it was introduced from Bangkok by accident. It's still around, but has not become as much of a problem as once feared.

The fish has air-breathing organs, and it propels itself by powerful pectoral spines. These spines can be very painful, so pick the fish up carefully the next time you see one walking across the road. The fish are edible, but they are hard to skin—and the skin stinks. Even so, this species is highly prized in Southeast Asia. It grows to 20-some-odd inches in length.

Grass Carp and White Amur

These fish have been stocked selectively in North America because they eat and help control aquatic plants. In some areas, they have become something of a problem. In Florida, these fish must be released because they were stocked for weed control and apparently will not reproduce. They grow up to 75 pounds.

Attempts have been made to find a market for the fish, but it's a hard sell in North America, partly because its flaky white meat is very bony. Anglers don't go for it either. A few are caught while fishing for catfish or other species, but most are caught when, if we may believe reports on television, they jump into speeding boats.

In any case, the grass carp is eaten in Asia, and in Laos they are consumed raw, thinly sliced, as an appetizer. I'll take a little Nuoc Cham dipping sauce (recipe in chapter 16) with mine.

Tilapia

Now a popular and inexpensive market fish, the tilapia was raised in ponds over two thousand years ago by the Egyptians. Today they are farmed in warm waters all around the world. In Florida, wild populations have been established in some areas and the fish is now sought out by a few avid anglers, mostly in urban areas. The bait? Small bread balls, dog food, and frankfurters.

The fish grows to 10 pounds or better. The mild white flesh is good—especially when freshly caught. The fillets are perfect for blackening (see the Blackened Crappie Fillets recipe in chapter 9).

Mayan Cichid

Sometimes called freshwater snapper, these panfish are also called atomic sunfish—and with good reason. They will hit a variety of artificial lures, including plugs and popping bugs. Weighing 2 pounds or a little better, they are native to Central and South America and have been established in parts of Florida since 1983.

There are no bag limits or size restrictions on this tasty fish . . . so catch all you want. The flesh is mild, white, flaky, and tasty.

Jaguar Guapote

Native to Central and South America, these fish are tolerant of poor-quality water, making them ideal for some Florida canals. Growing up to 16 inches long, it is caught on small artificial lures as well as live bait. It is purely excellent table fare.

Peacock Bass

This beautiful and great sport fish from Central and South America has become established in the canals and lakes in the Miami area. It is caught on baitcasting tackle, just like the largemouth, and it often hits large top-water plugs. It makes excellent table fare and can be cooked like largemouth bass.

Unlike most exotic species in American waters, the peacock was stocked by the state of Florida. It isn't likely to become established farther north of Miami because it can't survive in cooler waters.

As far as I am concerned, the peacock bass would be a good addition to almost any public fishing hole. Anglers who snort at this ought to remember that the brown trout is an "exotic," having been stocked in this country from Europe back in 1883. So . . . not all exotics are bad!

Smoked Fish Log (p. 148)

Angler's Lagniappe

Delectable White Roe, Dainty Fish Cheeks, Delicious Batarekh, and Other Gourmet Fare Free for the Eating

Every time I see a display of fish fillets in my local supermarket, I wonder what happened to the rest of the fish. Moreover, it's getting harder and harder these days to find fish that haven't been filleted. It's true that some fish markets offer whole fish, innards and all, but you have to wonder how long they have been out of water. Once again, I have to conclude that the angler has the best of the eating—free, if he wants to take advantage of it.

Here are some suggestions for using what I consider to be some of the best parts of the angler's catch—usually unavailable at market except possibly at exorbitant prices.

Roe

A lot of freshwater fish have very good roe, and some are better than anything on the market. Some freshwater fish, such as shad, have fine roe (small egglets) and, in general, these are my favorite. The very best roe I've ever eaten—and I've eaten a lot—is the roe of small bluegill and shellcracker.

Roe has been discussed in some of the previous chapters, along with a recipe or two. Some of the roe gets high marks in some cookbooks and culinary works, but for the most part this delicacy is largely unsung, partly because most of the freshwater fish are not available at market. Almost all freshwater fish have edible roe. Be warned, however, that the roe of some freshwater gars may be toxic to man, although they make excellent bluegill bait.

Here are some suggestions free for the eating.

Stuffed Shad Roe

This old Chesapeake Bay recipe is one of my favorite ways of cooking shad and mullet roe. It can also be used for other roe with tiny berries in large sacs.

- 8 roe sacs
- ½ pound lump crabmeat
- 1 stick butter
- 1 cup cream
- 2 tablespoons flour
- salt and pepper to taste

Preheat the oven to 350 degrees. Poach the roe sacs for 15 minutes. Drain and sauté in melted butter until browned. Drain on a brown bag. Add a little more butter to the skillet. Stir in the flour with a wooden spoon. Cook and stir, cook and stir, until you have a light roux. Slowly add the cream, stirring as you go, until you have a smooth sauce. Add the crabmeat and set aside.

Carefully split each roe sac lengthwise, but do not cut all the way through. Stuff the roe with the crab mixture. Put in the oven and heat for a few minutes. Serve hot, along with vegetables, hollandaise sauce (recipe in chapter 16), and biscuits.

Sautéed Large Roe

Many people fry large roe sacs, such as those from shad and mullet, and serve them up with the fried fish. This is convenient, but it really isn't the best way to go and can easily result in dry, crumbly fare. (The exception is small roe from bluegill and other small panfish.) It's best to first poach large roe sacs, then sauté them in butter.

roe sacs
salted butter
lemon
water

Put about an inch of water into a skillet. Add the roe sacs. Bring to a boil, cover, reduce the heat, and simmer until the water evaporates, turning from time to time. Add the butter and sauté for a few minutes. Sprinkle on some lemon juice. Plate the roe, add some chopped parsley to the skillet, and cook, stirring with a wooden spoon, for a few minutes. Pour the sauce over the roe and serve warm, along with lemon wedges.

A.D.'s Secret

A lady friend of a culinary bent once gave me a secret way to prevent large roe sacs from popping when fried in a skillet. Simply wrap them in aluminum foil and fry as usual, she said. Well, that will stop the grease splatter all right, and the result is okay. But the roe isn't really fried, it seems to me. In any case, I prefer my way of doing them, adding more flavor.

mullet or shad roe
bacon
water
salt and pepper

Put the roe sacs and bacon into a deep skillet and add enough water to cover by 1 inch. Bring to a boil, reduce the heat to low, and simmer until all the water has evaporated. By now the roe will be steamed done and a lot of the oil will have cooked out of the bacon.

Keep cooking, stirring around from time to time to keep the bottoms from burning. Sprinkle with a little salt and pepper, and cook until the bacon is crispy and the roe is well browned. Remove to drain. Serve the roe with the bacon, sliced tomatoes, green onions, and so on, along with some toast.

Easy Carp Caviar

Some epicures question the supreme status of Russian and Iranian caviar, and claim that the egglets from ordinary carp are hard to beat. Be sure to try it the next time you catch a fat sow. Here's a very easy recipe. The measures aren't exact—but don't cut back very much on the salt. Note that I make the caviar in a Crock-Pot for convenience. Other crockery will do, but avoid metal containers.

1 pound carp roe
½ cup salt
juice of 1 lemon
good water

Open the sacs and strip the egglets into a large bowl. Rinse well with cool water, using your hands to stir about. Drain and put into a Crock-Pot.

Mix a brine, using 1 quart of water, salt, and the lemon juice. Pour the brine over the roe, stirring with a wooden spoon. Cover and place in the refrigerator for 3 to 4 days.

Drain and eat with crackers or dark bread, and be sure to try the caviar as a topping for oysters on the half-shell.

Flemish-Style Roe

Wrap each roe sac in muslin. Put the roe into a pot with some salted water. Bring to a boil. Remove the roe and drain. Unwrap the roe and slice it carefully into ½-inch wheels. Sauté these in melted butter. Serve on toast, along with wedge of lemon.

Scrambled Eggs and Fish Roe

This is my favorite way to use a few roe when I don't have enough to cook as an entree.

Whisk the eggs. Remove the roe egglets from the sacs and stir into the eggs. Exact measures aren't necessary, but I like to have about half roe and half eggs by volume.

Melt a little butter in a skillet on medium heat. Sauté a few finely chopped scallions (with about half the green top). Pour in the egg mixture and scramble with a wooden spoon until the eggs are set. Serve hot, along with toast and crisp bacon.

Batarekh

When trying to encourage one of my young sons to try my dried mullet roe, I informed him that they were favorite noshing fare of the Pharaohs of ancient Egypt. "I don't want any," he said, turning his head. "They look like little mummies." Well, yes they did, and, I admit, they are something of an acquired taste.

These days, dried mullet roe, usually from France or Sardinia, is available commercially at very high prices, sold mostly to gourmets in New York, Paris, and other culinary hot spots. It is very expensive. I also understand that our Gulf of Mexico roe is being exported to Japan by the ton. They also dry it and sell it back to us at high prices. The old salts along the Outer Banks of North Carolina consider dried mullet roe common fare, and carry it around in their pockets.

In any case, dried roe is truly a treasure in my culinary life, and I wouldn't be able to afford it if I had to purchase it from New York. In addition to enjoying dried mullet roe as a snack or appetizer, I often use it as a seasoning, or grate it onto pizza as a topping. It will also kick up your bland au gratin.

The dried roe is easy to keep. Although some of the commercial roe is encased in a wax coating, I find this unnecessary and unpleasant. Simply put it into plastic bags and refrigerate. The vacuum-pack bags are ideal for long storage. Or, if you must, dip each piece in melted wax.

It's very easy to make batarekh if you have fresh mullet roe (which is available in the fall, not in the spring).

Lay the washed roe sacs on brown bags, salt them heavily, and put them in a dry, airy place. The salt will draw water out of the sacs, so change the bags after a few hours. Change again after a few more hours.

After several days, the roe will be dry and ready to eat. You'll know it's ready when the roe leaves no wet spot on the brown bag. Cut a sac in half and slice it thinly with a very sharp, thin knife. It should be tacky enough to hold together instead of crumbling like regular roe. Put the thin slice on a small cracker, add a drop of lemon juice, and enjoy.

White Roe

This delicacy, sometimes called soft roe, deserves a separate heading, partly because it is so good and because it is almost always thrown away. What, exactly, is it? If you don't know, don't ask. Although unmentionable, it is perfectly safe to eat. As a matter of fact, it is highly nutritious and easily digested.

I am partial to the white roe of mullet (partly because I can get plenty of it,) but male salmon, shad, carp, and some other fish have sacs of white roe. The roe should be fresh, but it can be refrigerated for a few days. And it freezes well. I freeze mine in water, but vacuum-sealed bags also work.

I've seen dozens of white roe recipes from *Larousse Gastronomique* and other culinary tomes, but the best method of cooking white roe is to simply sprinkle it with salt, dust it with flour, and fry it in bacon drippings or cooking oil. Or forget the flour and sauté it in butter.

Fish Heads

I once cooked one of my favorite fish dishes, Bass Veracruz (recipe in chapter 1), for several people with a nice 8-pounder. The head was all that was left, except for the backbone. I made a joke about giving the eyeballs to the guest of honor, but she wasn't much of a culinary sport, to say the least. When she returned to the table, I decided to leave the head untouched and unsung. The next day, when the house was empty, I heated the head and some of the pan drippings for my lunch, centering it on the plate. I had just started picking the head when my son came in and caught me. I asked him not to tell anybody. He said he wouldn't, but of course he told the whole town. After that, I made no attempt to hide my love of fish heads. Anyone who doesn't want to look at a head on the platter can sit at another table.

And I am not alone in my fondness for fish heads. In Asia, the heads of some fish are often sold separately at market. Snakefish heads are especially prized, and the head of the lowly carp contains one of the greatest of culinary tidbits enjoyed in Southeast Asia—an adenoid-like appendage found in the back of the throat.

On most fish, including the walleye, the cheeks, one on either side, are quite possibly the best meat on the fish. Don't laugh. In some markets, the cheeks of large saltwater fish, such as the halibut, can be purchased separately. Throats are also very good, and these too are sometimes marketed separately. I am especially fond of bass throats. These are the triangular piece of meat between the gill flaps and the pectoral fin. They can be removed during cleaning and cooked separately, but more often than not they are removed with the head—and thrown out. What a waste of good eating.

For the most part, eating the head is simply a matter of picking out the meat wherever you find it. Of course, fish heads can be used to make various soups, or they can be poached or baked with the rest of the fish.

I might add that I am also fond of nibbling on the heads of small fish, such as bluegills. Also, whenever I cook up a batch of bream, I also bread and fry a few of the smaller heads for my dog Nosher along with the hush puppies. That dog dearly loves a fish fry.

In any case, fish heads make excellent stocks (recipe in chapter 16) and soups. Here's one of my favorite recipes to try.

Long Island Fish Head and Oyster Soup

I found this recipe in J. George Frederick's *Long Island Seafood Cook Book.* Since Long Island oysters tend to be a little large, I have doubled the count, assuming smaller oysters will be used. I really prefer the smaller oysters, but suit yourself. (Some British writer has quipped that trying to eat a fat Long Island oyster was like trying to swallow a baby.)

4 fish heads (from 2- or 3-pound fish)
2 dozen fresh oysters (medium size)
1 cup whole milk or half-and-half
1 medium onion, chopped
1 carrot, chopped
1 tablespoon minced fresh parsley
1 tablespoon butter
1 tablespoon flour
6 peppercorns, ground
salt and pepper to taste
mace

Shuck the oysters, saving all the juice. Mix the juice with enough water to make 1 ½ quarts in a suitable pot. Add the fish heads, carrots, onions, peppercorns, and a pinch of mace. Bring to a boil, cover, and simmer for 2 hours. Remove the heads and strain the liquid into a pot. Flake all the meat off the heads and add it to the new pot, discarding the bones. Swirl in the butter and add the milk.

In a small saucepan, dissolve the flour in the oyster liquor, using a little water if needed. Stir the paste into the soup. Increase the heat, brining the soup to a light boil. Add the parsley, salt, and pepper. Add the oysters and simmer for 5 minutes. Serve hot with plenty of crackers. I'll take another twist or two of black pepper over mine.

Fish Ribs and Backbones

The rib cages and backbones of most fish contain some excellent meat. The backbone can be fried along with the fillets, or it can be used in soups and stews. The ribs can also be cooked in the same way, but I would also like to include a couple of other suggestions.

Carp Rib Finger Food

The ribs from large carp and other fish can be cut out in a slab and then cut into individual fingers. These will include a rib bone in the middle and a little meat on either side. Salt and pepper these, dust with flour or fine cornmeal, and fry in hot oil until browned and crispy. Serve as an appetizer. The trick is to hold the rib on the big end between the fingers and strip off the meat between your teeth. Serve with a good dipping sauce.

A.D.'s Vietnamese Chips

As discussed in chapter 11, I often cut the rib cages out of bluegill and other hand-shaped fish, including crappie, to make the fish fit better on the grill or in the skillet. The ribs are saved and cooked separately, and may be the best part.

Going one by one, place each rib on a heavy wooden chopping block. Using a dull meat cleaver, chop them across the ribs, but do not cut all the way through. If your cleaver is sharp, use the back side and pound the ribs. It is important to work them over good.

Heat peanut oil in your skillet to 375 degrees. Salt the ribs, dip them in flour or extra-fine cornmeal, and fry for a minute or two, until browned and crispy. If all has gone well, you can eat these bones and all. For an appetizer at a dinner party, call these Asian chips and serve with Nuoc Cham dipping sauce (recipe in chapter 16). Health-food freaks should also be advised that these chips are high in calcium.

Leftovers

Leftover fish should not be thrown out. Save them for the breakfast recipe, below, or for use in the flaked fish recipes set forth throughout this book. Fried, poached, baked, broiled, or grilled fish leftovers are all good. Here are a couple of suggestions.

Smoked Fish Log

Any good smoked fish can be used for this recipe, but I normally use hot-smoked mullet. Smoked whitefish would be even better. If you don't have smoked fish, add a little liquid smoke to regular fish flakes. Leftovers will do. Note, however, that the fish must be rather dry to keep the log firm. Otherwise, it may be difficult to slice. The pecans, popular in Texas cookery, are available in supermarkets.

- 2 cups flaked smoked fish
- 8-ounce package cream cheese
- ½ cup finely chopped pecans
- ½ cup chopped fresh parsley
- 1 tablespoon grated onion
- 1 tablespoon freshly squeezed lemon juice
- ½ tablespoon grated fresh horseradish
- salt to taste

Soften the cream cheese in a warm place. Mix it with the onion, horseradish, lemon juice, and salt. Mix in the fish flakes. Chill the mixture in the refrigerator for several hours.

When you are ready to proceed, mix the pecans and parsley. Shape the fish mixture into a log shape and carefully roll it in the pecans and parsley. Serve with assorted plain and fancy crackers. For a beer-drinking session, ordinary saltines will do, and you can omit the parsley.

Easy Fish Breakfast

This is one of my favorite ways to use leftover fish. It makes a hearty breakfast or a light lunch. One of the best ways to use up a small amount of leftover bass is to flake and scramble it with eggs for breakfast or brunch. Exact measures aren't necessary.

flaked fish
chicken eggs
scallions, chopped with part of green tops
butter
sea salt and freshly ground pepper

Whisk the eggs in a bowl and stir in the flaked fish. Sauté the chopped onions in butter for 5 minutes. Add the fish mixture and scramble until the eggs are set hard or soft, as you like 'em. It shouldn't be too dry, however. Salt and pepper to taste. Serve with bacon or ham, toast, and sliced vine-ripened tomatoes.

A.D.'s Fish Gravy Breakfast

After you fry a few fish for supper, leave the grease in the skillet and save any leftovers. The next morning, heat the grease and pour off the excess, leaving a tablespoon or so in the skillet. When the oil is hot, scrape up the little brown bits from the bottom. Add a little flour, a pinch or two at a time, and stir on low heat until you have a nice roux. Flake the leftover fish and add some to the gravy. Serve hot over biscuit halves or with grits and eggs. Enjoy.

Innards

I once knew a guy who ran a catfish trot line on a more-or-less commercial basis. He didn't really need the extra money to supplement his income, but the trot line was the only way he could easily catch enough cats to satisfy a culinary craving. You see, he loved the livers, which he usually fried along with a little bacon. A few other culinary sports have also expressed a fondness for fish liver (see The General's Choice recipe in chapter 7). But others find the very thought off-putting, to say the least. So . . . take 'em or leave 'em, depending on how sporty you are, culinarily speaking.

A few fish, such as mullet and gizzard shad, have an organ for grinding their food. This beautiful white muscle is edible, but it is also tough and lacking in flavor. Although I don't recommend fish gizzards as table fare, I always cook them when available, for a topic of conversation or for shock value, depending on who I am feeding.

One other innard is sometimes eaten. This is the swim bladder, or gas bladder. It is used by some fish as a flotation device and as a means of breathing air. I have eaten several swim bladders fried, but find them gelatinous and quite bland. These are not for me, but in Asia, fish bladders, sometimes from the swamp eel, are used in a soup. Anyone who can't resist the challenge can find a recipe, Nga-Si Phaung-Hin-Cho, in Alan Davidson's *Seafood of Southeast-East Asia*. Or, for openers, simply sauté a few bass or bullhead bladders and use them in the Fish Head and Oyster Soup, set forth earlier in this chapter.

What else? I have mentioned that mullet innards are sometimes eaten, but I offer no recipes. Anyone who shudders at the notion of eating such innards should stay away from small canned sardines, which are packed guts and all. And, be honest. Are not the plump fronts of the sardines more toothsome than the tail ends?

Cocktail Sauce (p. 156)

Fish Sauces, Stocks, and Go-Withs

A.D.'s Secret Oyster Juice Hush Puppies, Edible Cole Slaw, Homemade Tartar Sauce, Molbo Cru, and So On

This chapter really doesn't need much of an introduction, except to say that the success of a good fish supper or lunch often depends on good ingredients and helpful go-withs, plain and fancy, homemade and store-bought. Often, it really is the small things that matter most.

Here are a few recipes, notes, advice, and, I admit, a pet peeve or two. Some of the headings denote recipes, and others are for related topics. All of the recipes will, of course, have a list of ingredients.

Fish Stock

Normally, a fish stock is made without an exact recipe, and, all too often, the makings of a good fish stock are thrown out by the angler—and are unavailable to chefs who rely on the supermarket fish fillets. The vegetable ingredients can be varied, depending on what you have on hand. Celery is the only item I would buy especially for a fish stock.

- fish heads, ribs and backbones, trimmings
- celery and other fresh vegetables (onion, carrots, peppers)
- fresh herbs (parsley, cilantro, etc.)
- water

Put the fish parts, vegetables, and herbs into a pot and cover with water. Bring to a boil, reduce the heat, cover, and simmer for 30 minutes. Strain through cheesecloth and chill until needed. Most people will throw out the spent heads and frames, but I like to nibble on any remaining meat tidbits.

If you have shellfish trimmings at hand, be sure to add them to the pot along with the fish parts. Shrimp heads make an outstanding stock. Note also that the stock can be diluted if it seems too strong.

For a stock to be used as poaching liquid, see the next recipe.

Court Bouillon

This ten-dollar term is simply a liquid used for poaching fish. It's best to cook the court bouillon and then cool it before reheating to poach the fish. Make it a day or two ahead of time and put it into the refrigerator until needed.

After you poach a few fish in the court bouillon, you can reduce the liquid and use it as a fish stock. Or as a broth.

Heat a quart or two of water to the boil. Add some chopped onions, carrots, and celery with the tops. (I always use the large outer ribs of celery because the inner ribs are better for the raw salad or for stirring the Bloody Mary.) Various fresh herbs, or a bouquet garni, can be used, along with a little salt and pepper. Add, if you like, wine, lemon juice, or vinegar in reasonable amounts.

Mongol Tartar Sauce

The name for tartar sauce, and for beef tartare, came from the Tartar Mongol people who settled beyond the steppes of Eurasia. In addition to being used for fish dishes, it was also served with venison and smoked meat. This recipe, made with yogurt and a little horseradish, is quite tasty and highly recommended for those who want something a little different.

- yolks of 6 hard-boiled eggs
- 2 tablespoons plain yogurt
- 2 tablespoons olive oil
- 2 tablespoons finely chopped dill pickles
- 1 tablespoon grated horseradish
- 1 tablespoon red wine vinegar
- ½ tablespoon mustard
- ½ tablespoon honey

Mash the egg yolks in a bowl. Thoroughly mix in the other ingredients, put into a suitable jar, and refrigerate until needed.

A.D.'s Secret-Ingredient Tartar Sauce

Every jackleg chef ought to have a secret recipe for tartar sauce. Here's mine. Note that the secret ingredients are always revealed at the dinner table. If you don't have the ingredient at hand, lie like a Texan. It's the thought that counts.

- 1 cup good mayonnaise (preferably homemade)
- ¼ cup minced scallions with half the green tops
- ¼ cup minced red bell pepper
- ¼ cup minced gherkin pickles
- ¼ cup minced green olives
- 1 tablespoon minced capers (optional)
- 2 fire ants
- lemon juice to taste
- fresh dill weed to taste
- salt and white pepper to taste

Mash the dill weed and ants together with a mortar and pestle. Set aside. Mix all the other ingredients and let set for a few minutes. Taste. Stir in a little dill weed and secret ingredient to taste. Set aside for a while before using, letting the flavors mingle.

Low-Fat Tartar Sauce

Here's a tasty recipe without much fat. If you want more fat, use a full cup of homemade mayonnaise and omit the yogurt.

½ cup low-fat mayonnaise
½ cup low-fat yogurt
2 tablespoons finely chopped salad pickles
2 tablespoons minced scallions
juice and grated zest of 1 lemon
1 clove garlic, mashed and minced
1 tablespoon finely chopped fresh parsley
1 teaspoon prepared yellow mustard

When you mince the onions, be sure to include about half the green tops. Mix all ingredients in a bowl. Transfer to a serving container and refrigerate for an hour or so before serving.

Maître D'Hôtel Sauce

This popular sauce works as a table condiment as well as for basting fish during the last few minutes of broiling and grilling.

¼ cup butter
juice of 1 lemon
grated zest of 1 lemon
1 tablespoon minced fresh parsley
½ teaspoon salt
⅛ teaspoon white pepper

Soften the butter and whip it in a small bowl. Stir in the salt, pepper, lemon zest, and parsley. Slowly, drop by drop, stir in the lemon juice. Serve at room temperature.

Lemon Butter

Use lemon butter as a baste for grilled or broiled fish, and as a dipping condiment on the table. This sauce is very good for fish fingers and boiled shrimp. It is much thinner than the Maître D'Hôtel Sauce above.

½ cup butter
¼ cup freshly squeezed lemon juice
finely grated zest of a lemon or two
2 tablespoons minced fresh parsley
1 clove minced garlic

Melt the butter in a saucepan. Add the other ingredients, cooking and stirring for 5 minutes on low heat to mingle the flavors. (Do not boil.) Go ahead. Stick your finger in it and have a taste.

Avgolémono Sauce

This Greek sauce is often used with soups. It can be made with chicken stock, fish stock, or part of the soup.

- 2 eggs at room temperature
- juice of 2 lemons
- 1 cup hot fish stock

Beat the eggs and gradually stir in the lemon juice. Then stir in the hot fish stock. Use with fish sews and soups.

Ata Sauce

Here's a hot pepper sauce from West Africa. How hot is it? Much depends on your choice of chile pepper. I use jalapeños because they are widely available. Much also depends on how well you take the innards out of the hot peppers. The heat is in the inner veins as well as the seeds. The ground dried shrimp are essential to the dish, and can be purchased in some ethnic markets.

- 5 red bell peppers, seeded and chopped
- 3 or 4 jalapeño peppers, seeded and chopped
- 2 large tomatoes, chopped
- 1 large onion, chopped
- ½ cup peanut oil
- 1 teaspoon ground dried shrimp
- salt to taste

Zap all of the peppers, onion, and tomatoes in a blender. Heat the peanut oil in a stove-top Dutch oven or suitable pot. Add the blender contents and sauté for 10 minutes or so. Add the ground shrimp and fry on low heat, stirring as you go with a wooden spoon, until the sauce is lightly browned. Do not burn.

Molbo Cru

This sauce from Angola goes nicely over poached fish fillets, or as a dip for fried fish fingers. Be sure to use whole cumin seeds and grind them in your mortar and pestle.

- 1 cup diced green tomatoes
- ½ cup vinegar
- ¼ cup chopped fresh parsley
- 4 garlic cloves, pressed
- 1 tablespoon freshly ground cumin seeds
- ½ teaspoon sea salt
- ½ cup water

Put all the ingredients into a food processor or blender. Zap it until you have a smooth paste. Chill in the refrigerator before serving.

Walnut Sauce

Walnut sauce is popular in the Republic of Georgia, and I like it with good American fish. It goes best with lean white fish (see the recipe for Walleye with Indian Rice in chapter 4). Here's what you'll need:

- ½ cup chopped walnuts
- 1 cup thinly sliced mushrooms
- 2 cups half-and-half
- ¼ cup butter
- ¼ cup white flour
- 2 tablespoons minced onion
- ½ teaspoon dry mustard
- ½ teaspoon dried thyme
- salt and white pepper to taste

Carefully toast the walnuts in a dry cast-iron skillet, being very careful not to burn. (This is a hands-on job, snaking the skillet as you go.) When toasted, dump the nuts onto a plate and set aside.

Melt the butter in the skillet. Sauté the mushrooms and onions for 5 minutes. Mix in the flour and cook, stirring as you go (with a wooden spoon) until you have a light roux. Stir in the thyme, mustard, salt, and white pepper to taste. Mix in the walnuts and transfer to a sauce bowl. Serve warm with baked fish.

Dill Sauce

This sauce is best made with fresh dill weed from your garden. It is also available from some supermarkets these days.

- 2 cups sour cream
- juice of 2 lemons
- zest of 2 lemons (finely grated)
- 1 tablespoon minced fresh dill
- ½ teaspoon sea salt

Mix all the ingredients and refrigerate for several hours, letting the flavors blend. Serve cold with chilled poached fish.

Mustard-Dill Sauce

This sauce is recommended for gravlax (recipe in chapter 3), but it is also tasty with other dishes. Try it as a last-minute baste for grilled salmon.

- 1 cup Dijon or good brown mustard
- 3 tablespoons olive oil
- 2 tablespoons white wine vinegar
- 1 tablespoon sugar
- ¼ cup minced fresh dill weed
- ½ teaspoon white pepper
- salt to taste

Using a whisk, mix the mustard, sugar, and pepper in a small bowl. Whisking briskly as you go, slowly mix in part of the olive oil, pouring in a thin stream. Mix in a little of the wine vinegar. Repeat with oil and wine vinegar until used up. Add a little salt to taste. Last, mix in the dill weed. Refrigerate until you are ready to serve.

Catsup, Catchup, or Ketchup

Regardless of how you spell it, tomato-based ketchup (and, yes, there can be other kinds, such as mushroom) is an indispensable condiment for the American table. The British brought a ketchup sauce from India, but the sauce as we now know it is New England's contribution to American cookery. In any case, homemade tomato ketchup is not practical these days, what with so many good brands available at the supermarket.

It is conventional to serve ketchup on the table in a bottle. This can cause some problems in getting the stuff out. The new upside-down squirt bottles are all right, I guess, but can cause some suggestive noises at the table. For formal use, I recommend serving the ketchup in small individual bowls. But most people will want a blob on the plate for easy dipping.

Salsa

Tomato-based salsa has become one of the more popular condiments in America. Normally used as a dip, it is also useful as an ingredient in recipes and as a fish sauce for the table. Fortunately, it is available hot, medium, and mild—so get a jar for everyone.

Of course, homemade salsa can also be used to advantage, along with, in some cases, such creations as mango salsa.

Cocktail Sauce

This is a great sauce for dipping fried fish fingers and cold poached fish or "mock shrimp."

- 1 cup ketchup
- juice of 1 large lemon
- 2 tablespoons red wine
- 1 large clove garlic
- 1 tablespoon olive oil
- 1 tablespoon freshly grated horseradish
- ½ teaspoon Tabasco sauce
- ¼ teaspoon sea salt

Using a garlic press or blade of a meat cleaver, crush the garlic and put it into 1 tablespoon of olive oil. Let it steep for 2 or 3 days. Strain off the oil into a small mixing bowl and discard the garlic. Stir in the rest of the ingredients. Chill for a few hours before serving.

A.D.'s Highly Secret Red Sauce

Here's my secret red sauce, which I usually serve with fried oysters. It's also good with fried fish fingers, used as a dip. Finely grated fresh horseradish root is the real secret. The green tomato worm puree is a decoy.

- 2 cups good red tomato ketchup
- 2 tablespoons finely grated horseradish
- ⅛ teaspoon green tomato worm puree

Put the ketchup in a mixing bowl and stir in some finely grated horseradish root. Stir it in a little at a time, tasting as you go, until you get it as you like it. Serve as a dip for deep fried fish fingers or fillets. Be sure to throw out the tomato worm puree.

Mustard Sauce

This sauce can be used as a baste or a dip, but it's really best when poured over poached fish, either on the serving platter or on individual plates. Although I normally use ordinary yellow mustard, gourmet chefs may want to use instead brown mustard, Creole mustard, or whatever. Just keep the "mustard" in the name of the recipe. If you choose to use red wine instead of white, I won't tell anybody.

- 2 cups fish stock
- ¼ cup butter
- ¼ cup half-and-half
- ½ cup white wine
- 2 tablespoons prepared mustard
- 2 tablespoons all-purpose flour
- salt and white pepper to taste

Melt the butter in a small saucepan and stir in the flour a little at the time. When you have a light roux, stir in the fish stock slowly. Salt and pepper to taste. Cook and stir for 10 minutes or so. Stir in the wine. Stir in the mustard and half-and-half. Keep warm but do not boil. Serve hot in a gravy boat, letting each partaker spoon the sauce over their serving of fish.

Easy Fried-Fish Dipping Sauce

This sauce goes with any nicely fried fish, preferably small strips served as finger food. Use regular soy sauce, not that low-sodium stuff.

- ½ cup chicken broth
- ½ cup soy sauce
- juice of 1 lemon

Mix the ingredients in a small saucepan. Bring to heat, but do not boil, stirring as you go. Remove from the heat and steep for a few minutes. Go ahead. Stick your finger in it and have a taste. Serve warm.

Nuoc Cham

This Vietnamese dipping sauce is one of my favorite table condiments for fried finger foods. Any good Asian fish sauce will do, but the Vietnamese Nuoc Nam is authentic. Nuoc Cham should be made fresh for every meal, using a mortar and pestle. It's truly worth the labor.

It is best made with a fresh red chile pepper. I prefer jalapeños ripened on the stalk in my garden. Fresh cherry peppers also work. Dried red peppers, or pepper flakes, can also be used, if necessary.

- ¼ cup Nuoc Nam or other Asian fish sauce
- 2 cloves garlic
- hot red chile pepper
- 1 tablespoon sugar
- ¼ fresh lime
- a little water as needed

Peel and mince the garlic. Seed, devein, and mince the chile pepper. Put the garlic, red pepper, and sugar into a mortar. Pound into a paste with the pestle. Squeeze the lime juice into the mix, and add the pulp from the lime. Add the fish sauce and mash everything together, using a little water as necessary to thin the sauce. Serve as a dipping sauce or condiment at room temperature.

Homemade Mayonnaise

Freshly squeezed lemon juice is the key to a good mayonnaise. Most of the commercial brands fall short in this regard. Most of them contain no real lemon at all. Nada. The difference between mayonnaise and salad dressing is not clear to me—or anybody else.

In any case, I recommend that you make small batches of mayonnaise and use it right away. Anything made with uncooked chicken eggs and stored for any length of time can cause a salmonella bloom. So, make it as needed.

Any good cooking oil can be used, but I strongly recommend a good olive oil. A blender or food processor can be used if you need a large batch, but for a small batch you need only a small bowl and a fork, making the cleanup easy.

1 cup olive oil
1 egg yolk
1 tablespoon freshly squeezed lemon juice
1 tablespoon white vinegar
½ teaspoon dry mustard

All the ingredients, the fork, and the bowl should be very cold. Break up the egg yolk in a bowl with the spoon. Add a little of the lemon juice. Drop by drop, whisk in the olive oil, stirring constantly and adding the rest of the ingredients as you go. Have a taste with your finger and refrigerate the rest until serving time.

A.D.'s Hollandaise from Scratch

Store-bought hollandaise is usually acceptable, but it is so easy to make your own as needed. As with mayonnaise, the key is fresh lemon juice. The lemon zest is a bonus.

When I was a kid on a farm, one of our hens laid very large eggs—and sometimes they had two yolks. These were reddish in color, and, since the hens were free to scratch for grubs and things, were full of protein. These days most of us have to rely on eggs from the supermarket.

2 large egg yolks
4 tablespoons melted butter (divided)
1 medium lemon
½ teaspoon fine sea salt
⅛ teaspoon cayenne

Using a coarse grater, scrape the zest off the lemon, avoiding the bitter white pith. Set aside. Beat the egg yolks in a small bowl until they thicken. Mix in the salt and cayenne. A little at a time, beat in 3 tablespoons of the melted butter. Mix the rest of the butter and the lemon juice in a small bowl. Combine the mixtures in the top of a double boiler and cook over hot water, stirring as you go, until the hollandaise thickens. Serve with fish and go-withs.

Yogurt Sauce

Here's an impromptu sauce that I used to make whenever my wife went on a yogurt-and-cucumber diet.

1 cup plain low-fat yogurt
1 tablespoon tupelo honey
8 drops of Tabasco sauce, or to taste

Mix the yogurt and honey, then stir in the Tabasco sauce one drop at the time to taste. Use as a finishing sauce over grilled or broiled fish.

Cajun Dust

I use this primarily for blackened fish, but it also comes in handy in other recipes. These days, blackening seasoning mixes can be purchased in the supermarket, and these are all right, I guess. For my purposes, however, they are all too spicy. Too hot to use in volume. I want a thick spice crust on my blackened fish, and I don't want it too hot. The trick is to add lots of powdered ancho pepper, which I purchase by the pound and use it to put the red in chili and buffalo stews. Mild paprika can be substituted for the ancho—and, if the truth be told, much of the paprika sold in North America is not Hungarian. It's simply ancho powder.

See also my Blackened Crappie Fillets recipe in chapter 9.

- 3 tablespoons red ancho powder
- 1 tablespoon cayenne
- 1 tablespoon black pepper
- 1 tablespoon onion powder
- 1 tablespoon fine sea salt
- 1 teaspoon powdered thyme
- 1 teaspoon powdered oregano

Mix all the ingredients and keep dry until needed for blackening fish or rubbing ribs at the barbecue. Sprinkle a little over a serving of scrambled eggs for a little flavor and color. A light sprinkle will quickly convert ordinary french fries to Cajun fries.

Twice-Fried French Fries

Although the old menu of fried fish, fried hush puppies, and fried potatoes might be a bit much for some modern health-food freaks, it sure is good. Since many people will serve french fries anyway, we might as well do it right. This involves frying the potatoes twice, a method that fits right in with a fish fry.

Use large Idaho or russet potatoes.

- 1 medium to large potato for each person
- peanut or vegetable oil for deep-frying
- salt to taste
- ketchup (optional)

Peel the potatoes if you must. French them into slender fingers. Soak them in cold water while you rig for deep-frying.

Heat 3 or more inches of peanut oil in a Dutch oven or other suitable pot or oblong fish fryer to a temperature of 325 degrees. Turn up the heat to maintain the temperature while you add the potatoes a few at a time. Lower the heat when your thermometer shows 325 again. Cook the fries for 10 minutes, stirring a time or two. Remove to drain.

At this point, they will be limp but not very brown. These can be set aside for up to an hour or so while you fry the hush puppies and fish, or you can proceed immediately. Heat the oil to 375 degrees. Put the potatoes back into the pot and fry for 2 minutes or so, until they are nicely brown and crisp. Drain on brown bags and sprinkle with salt. Serve hot along with the fish and hush puppies.

Have some ketchup on the table for those who want it.

A.D.'s Irish Fries

Here's a good skillet recipe to cook in camp as well as at home. I like to use new potatoes or red potatoes for these, but any small spud will do. Slice them 3⁄16 inch thick. A quarter of an inch is too much, and an eighth is not enough.

- sliced potatoes
- bacon drippings or cooking oil
- salt
- mild paprika (optional)

Heat ¼ inch of oil in a skillet. Fry the potatoes a few at a time for a few minutes on each side, until tender and a little browned. Drain on a brown bag. Sprinkle lightly with sea salt. A little mild paprika or ancho powder sprinkled on the top will improve the appearance, and won't hurt a thing.

Baked Beans

More and more we are seeing baked beans served at fish fries, partly, I suppose, to replace fried potatoes. I certainly approve the practice—if the beans are good. True Boston baked beans are by far the best, but are a little too much trouble for the average angler throwing a fish fry. Some canned beans are acceptable, but ordinary "pork and beans" leave a lot to be desired.

Most canned beans can be improved with a little cast-iron skillet magic. Sauté some chopped bacon in a skillet until nicely browned. Drain. Add some minced onion to the bacon drippings and cook until it starts to brown around the edges. Add a little dark brown sugar and heat until melted, stirring as you go with a wooden spoon. Dump a can of beans into the skillet and add the reserved bacon bits. Cook and stir, cook and stir, until the "bean juice" from the can is reduced. Serve hot.

A.D.'s Hominy & Salsa Combo

A lot of people in the Florida Panhandle where I live serve grits with fried fish. I think this goes back to the time when country people often served salt mullet for breakfast. (These were available in all country stores, sold from open wooden boxes, and on rolling stores.) The salt mullet were a little strong—and very salty. Mild grits helped tame the fish, and the tradition of grits-and-fish continued after modern refrigeration pretty much killed the salt-mullet industry.

Since I don't care for grits, I have substituted whole-kernel hominy, also made from corn. Old-timers made hominy in large batches, often in the butter churn, but modern cooks can purchase it canned at the supermarket. It is available in white or yellow. Use both.

Drain the hominy well and toss the kernels about to separate. Mix white and yellow in equal amounts in a serving bowl. Have ready a smaller bowl of tomato-based salsa—a very popular condiment these days, available in hot, medium, or mild. If in doubt, offer all three to your guests.

To serve, spoon a helping of hominy onto individual plates, then top with a little of the salsa. The combination of spicy salsa and mild hominy goes nicely with fried fish, and it is a very attractive dish.

The Almost Quintessential Hush Puppy

Every jackleg cook has a favorite hush puppy recipe, and I am no exception. Most people will add all manner of stuff to a standard "fried mush" batter, and the recipes tend to get longer and longer year by year. After all, the easiest way to have your own private recipe is to take another cook's creation and add a pinch of this and dash of that that to the ingredients list.

I, however, being whatever I am, have gone against the grain—back to the basics. I use only ground white cornmeal. This is made from a soft white whole-kernel corn, whereas most of the supermarket meal has the germ removed. Why? Because it contains some oil and tends to turn rancid in time, thereby decreasing the shelf life.

Owing to commercial practicality, whole-grain cornmeal almost disappeared from American cookery. It survived in parts of the South and, thank God, in Rhode Island. Today it is becoming more widely available, even in supermarkets. Remember that true whole-kernel meal should be stored in the refrigerator or, better, in the freezer.

So . . . getting the right stuff is the big problem. Once you get the right meal, the hush puppies are easy. Here's all you need.

- white whole-kernel cornmeal, fine or extra fine
- salt
- warm water
- oil for frying

Dump some cornmeal into a bowl, add a little salt, and pour in some warm water. Using your hands, mix until you have a nice batter, just a tad thicker than pancake batter. Add some salt and let the mix sit for 20 minutes or longer.

Heat a little oil in a skillet or deep-fryer. Drop the batter by the spoonful into the grease and cook until the hush puppies are nicely browned. If you are using a deep-fryer, these will be kind of round-ish, but if you are using a skillet the batter will tend to flatten out when it touches the bottom. I much prefer mine to flatten a little, which makes for a thinner and crisper bread, although it does, I admit, deviate from the popular notion that hush puppies tend to be round in shape. My dog Nosher will eat them either way, provided they are made with fresh white meal. Yellow meal, she says, is unfit for canine consumption.

A.D.'s Secret and Nosher's Favorite

Although the recipe above is, in my opinion, the original old-time hush puppy, unadorned by spices and such, I confess to embellishing the recipe—thereby elevating it to dog heaven. The secret?

Buy a sack of fresh oysters and save the juice when you shuck them for raw consumption on the half shell. The juice is the secret, but don't tell anybody. Use it in the previous recipe instead of the water, or along with the water if needed.

Redneck and Good Ol' Boy Hush Puppies

This variation, using beer, is for those who are too lazy or too drunk to shuck their own oysters. Though simple, the recipe is under constant contention, as one good ol' boy will want Budweiser and another will want Mexican Tepache or even even Lowenbrau. Guinness Stout, however, is a little strong for most tastes.

Take any good hush puppy recipe and mix the ingredients with beer. Make the batter and fry as usual, using no water whatsoever. Have more beer for drinking.

Yankee Hush Puppies

Mark Twain once said that Yankees don't know how to make good cornbread. They may think they know, he went on, but they really don't. I agree with Twain, but these days I must add that a lot of misguided Southerners and Midwesterners also use yellow meal. (I don't even want to get started on cornbread made west of the Mississippi, where, my God, they even use blue cornmeal.) Let me add, however, that I have never met a hush puppy that I didn't like, as Will Rodgers said. (If Will didn't say it, he ought to have.) Anyhow, here is a typical hush puppy recipe, using baking powder, chicken egg, and other stuff in addition to the basics of cornmeal, water, and salt.

1 ½ cups yellow cornmeal
½ cup white flour
1 cup milk
1 chicken egg, beaten
3 scallions, minced with part of green tops
1 tablespoon baking powder
1 teaspoon salt
black pepper or cayenne to taste
½ teaspoon dried sage
vegetable oil for deep-frying

Mix all the dry ingredients in a suitable bowl. Stir in the milk, scallions, and egg. Set aside. When you are ready to cook, heat the oil in a Dutch oven or deep fryer to 375 degrees. Using a spoon (which is dipped from time to time in water), drop the batter into the hot oil. Do not overcrowd. When the hush puppies are nicely browned and crusty, remove to drain. Fry and drain another batch, and so on. Serve hot or warm with fried fish.

Crazy Charley's Beer Batter

Many good ol' boys like to use beer in a batter recipe. Here's one from Charley Addison, Cajun.

¾ cup Bisquick
⅓ cup warm beer
2 chicken egg whites
1 teaspoon cooking oil
1 teaspoon salt
1 teaspoon black pepper
½ teaspoon garlic powder

Whisk the egg whites until stiff. Mix with the rest of the ingredients. Use as a batter for frying fish, broccoli, or, Crazy Charley says, anything worth frying.

Cornbread Stuffing or Dressing

Many recipes for chicken or turkey stuffings or dressings will work with baked fish. Here's an easy one to try. Use any good cornbread or corn muffin. Some stuffing recipes call for sage and other spices, some of which you may want to omit from a fish recipe.

- 2 cups crumbled cornbread
- 2 tablespoons minced onion
- 2 tablespoons minced celery
- 2 tablespoons minced red bell peppers
- 1 tablespoon minced green scallion tops
- ½ tablespoon Worcestershire sauce
- 1 chicken egg, whisked
- milk
- salt and pepper to taste

Mix all the ingredients, using enough milk to moisten the stuffing nicely. Refrigerate until you are ready to cook the fish, but use within a few hours.

Dusting for Fried Fish

In America, wheat flour and cornmeal are usually used to coat fish for frying. Both white and yellow cornmeal can be used, or blue, but a fine grind and soft texture may be more important than color. Fine or extra-fine flour or meal can be used directly on fish without much of a problem, but the gritty yellow meal from modern supermarkets doesn't stick too well and can cause problems with accumulation in the bottom of the fryer, especially at large cookouts. That's why lots of folks dip their fish in lightly whipped chicken egg, buttermilk, or some such goo before dusting.

One good technique for a crispy fry is to dip the fish first in flour (which tends to become sticky, like library paste), then in egg, and, finally in cornmeal or cracker crumbs.

Some people use the Japanese panko for a coating, and others use Jewish matzo meal, and, of course, various combinations are also used. Also, it's not uncommon to use pecan meal, walnut meal, and so on. Also try combinations of meal, ground nuts, and bread crumbs. Variations are endless.

The fish can be rolled in cornmeal or flour, but I prefer to shake mine. Put the meal into a container of some sort, add the fish, shake up and down, and then knock the excess from each piece when you take it out. Ordinary brown bags from the supermarket are ideal for shaking, and can be used to drain the fish, hush puppies, or french fries.

Some people will want to add a little salt and pepper to the flour or meal before shaking, but I think it is better to salt the fish and let it sit for a few minutes before dusting. The salt draws out a little moisture and helps stick the meal or flour.

Also, I sometimes flop fillets in olive oil before the dusting. This makes for a nice crust on the fish. It also helps stick the coating if the dusted fish are set aside, or refrigerated, for a while before frying.

Cooking Oil

I prefer peanut oil for deep-frying, partly because it stands up to high heat without smoking. Frugal cooks may want to strain the oil after a fry and use it again, or several times, as I do. Others may want to substitute a cheaper vegetable oil and throw it out after use. Both corn and canola oils are also good for deep-frying.

For sautéing in a skillet, bacon drippings or lard is hard to beat, but any good oil will do. I have been leaning toward olive oil in recent years. Butter is often used for the sauté, but it tends to burn easily. Clarified butter works much better, but camp cooks (who often use butter to sauté the trout) will prefer to mix in a little Crisco or other frying oil, as in the Trout Hemingway recipe in chapter 2.

Cole Slaw

Every jackleg cook has a recipe for cole slaw, calling for all manner of herbs, pickles, and stuff. Most of these are okay, I guess, but the recipe isn't as important as the other details, as demonstrated in my favorite recipe, adapted from *Better Homes and Garden's Heritage Cookbook* and reported in my column for *Gray's Sporting Journal.* The recipe is of Dutch origin and is quite old, going back to New Amsterdam, as Manhattan was once called. The measures can be increased as needed.

This simple, fresh-made approach, I must add, goes against advice from a popular cookbook writer, who adds all manner of stuff and advises us to let the cole slaw sit for several hours to let the flavors blend. Don't do it. If the cole slaw sits too long, the juices will accumulate to the bottom. This is especially bad if lots of cheap mayonnaise was used in the recipe, as is usually the case, and if the cole slaw is served cafeteria style. In many cases, new cole slaw is dumped into the batch, making even more juice at the bottom. So, if you are the last in line you may want to skip the cole slaw. It will not only be sickening (at least to me) but will also run into your fish, beans, or whatever else is on the plate.

- 1 quart shredded cabbage
- ½ cup heavy top milk (cream)
- 3 tablespoons apple cider vinegar
- 2 tablespoons sugar
- ¾ teaspoon salt
- ⅛ teaspoon freshly ground black pepper

Shortly before you are ready to eat, mix the cream, cider vinegar, sugar, salt, and pepper. Mix into the cabbage with your hands and toss thoroughly. Serve immediately.

Sliced Tomatoes

Good vine-ripened tomatoes are hard to beat with fried fish. Simply slice them about ¼ inch thick or a little better, and serve on a platter on the table, or on individual plates if you are serving cafeteria style. A little sea salt ground on from a salt mill, one slice at a time to taste, really hits the spot. To me, this is the best possible go-with for fried fish—if you have good home-grown, vine-ripened tomatoes.

Streamside Salad

A lot of anglers enjoy looking for mushrooms and other wild edibles along the water's edge. Those who don't are missing some very good eating, including fiddleheads, catbrier tips, Cossack asparagus, watercress, and so on. I would, however, recommend that culinary sports do their homework before eating this stuff—especially mushrooms.

- edible wild mushrooms
- scallions or wild onions (or ramps)
- olive oil
- wine vinegar
- salt and black pepper to taste
- salted water to boil

Clean and slice some wild mushrooms. Chop with scallions or wild onions, including the lower third of the green stems. Mix a salad dressing consisting of two parts olive oil and one part wine vinegar, along with a little salt and pepper.

Bring some water to boil in a pan. Add the mushrooms and cook for a few minutes. Drain and put in salad bowls for serving. While still hot, toss with some of the dressing. Sprinkle with chopped scallions and serve at once as a side to your catch of the day.

Aspic

Many are the recipes for salmon or other fish in aspic. These are always, of necessity, served cold, and are, in my opinion, much more suited to a buffet than to the dinner table. Some of the quick recipes use gelatin from the supermarket, but the better ones will be made from fish stock or court bouillon made with lots of fish bones, which will congeal naturally. Most recipes will call for white wine, but I say that rosé makes a prettier aspic.

I consider all the aspic dishes more suitable for chefs and food stylists catering to a rather swanky clientele, and will be of little use to anglers who cook their catch for home or camp consumption. I have therefore decided not to include a full-blown recipe and decorating instructions for aspic-encased fish in this unprissified book. It's my book—and, to be honest, I simply don't like the stuff, except maybe in Jell-O.

—Good Fishing, Good Cooking, and Good Eating—

Appendix I

Dressing and Caring for the Catch

The angler has the opportunity to put better fish on the table simply by taking good care of the catch. Although fish stringers, live wells, and creels all have their place, the best way to keep the fish fresh is to put them on ice as soon as possible. Hence, a good ice chest for the boat is one of the best investments an angler can make.

Gutting the catch is not as important (for most species) as some of us think, as long as the fish are quite cold. If the fish are kept on ice, the gutting can wait for a day or two. If frozen, for months. Honest.

Actually, a slush is better than regular ice. This works by sprinkling salt onto the ice. The salt makes the ice melt, and, in order to melt, it draws heat from the fish. This method is often used in salt water, where quick cooling of some species is necessary. With some sharks, for example, uric acid starts to form within minutes if the carcass isn't cooled down quickly. If you want to use this method, get some rock salt used for making ice cream at home.

Freezing the Catch. Many people prefer to freeze fish in water in 2-quart milk cartons or other suitable containers. I approve the practice, and I use the method to freeze fillets as well as small bluegill. In recent years, however, I have leaned more and more toward freezing the fish whole, guts and all, unscaled. This gives me the ability to cook the fish whole, filleted, or pan-dressed, depending on the recipe to be used.

It's easy. Simply freeze the fish separately, unwrapped. Once frozen, large fish can be sprayed with water mist and quickly put back into the freezer. This gives a coating of ice over the scales and skin—and that's about as good as you can do. The frozen innards won't hurt a thing, and can be discarded when the fish are dressed, or perhaps used in one way or another.

Not long ago, I acquired about 50 frozen scorpionfish from a large seafood outfit. To my surprise, and delight, they were frozen whole, undressed, and my guess is that they were sold to various fish markets in the same form. So . . . perhaps the fillets displayed so cleanly might well have been cut from fish that had first been frozen whole! Personally, I would like to see more whole-frozen fish in our markets. This would provide some good eating for those of us in the know, and would help preserve the old culinary ways of using all of the fish. This is not merely a matter of being frugal. It will lead to better cooking and better eating. Having the makings of a good fish stock will greatly improve many recipes.

I must also admit that perhaps I like the method of freezing the whole fish, unscaled and ungutted, because I am too lazy to clean them properly after a hard day's fishing. To hell with it, I say, after dragging in after dark. Put 'em in the freezer and have a beer. We'll thaw and clean the things when we get ready to cook.

In any case, I leave the frozen whole fish uncovered, stacked in my freezer like stove wood, until needed for a recipe. That way I'll at least be able to tell what's what, which isn't always the case when I wrap the fish in freezer paper. Smaller fish, such as bluegills, are frozen separately and then put into a large plastic bag.

I have kept whole frozen fish up to a year without any noticeable loss of texture and flavor, but most experts will recommend a much shorter freezer time. Much will depend on the condition of the fish at the time of freezing.

Scaling. Scaling the fish is best accomplished with a kitchen spoon. A commercial scaler can be used, but a spoon is better, at least for me. A knife with a stout blade can be used, but it is far from ideal.

To scale a fish, simply start at the tail and work toward the head. The scales will knock off easily with most fish, provided that they are fresh and still wet. If they dry out, the scaling will be tougher. A few fish, such as yellow perch, are rather difficult to scale, but these are the exception.

Skinning. Start by cutting a small slit behind the head. With the tip of the knife, loosen the skin enough to get a grip. If necessary, pinch the skin between the knife blade and the forefinger and pull down. This is much easier if you have pliers at hand, but these will quickly clog up with mucus from the skin and slip. By far the best bet is to purchase a pair of skinning pliers, available at tackle shops for a couple of bucks. These are really pincers and they grab the skin firmly without slipping. I wouldn't want to skin lots of catfish or eels without these. (By the way, nailing the catfish or eel head to a tree before skinning is usually a waste of time. Eels are really easy to skin if you can get a good grip on them, and I have worked out an easy way of combining the skinning with filleting, discussed a little later.)

Actually, skinning the fish is often done during the filleting process, second method, under the filleting section a little later.

Removing the Fins? A tail and fin nibbler, I seldom trim the fish before cooking them. Those who do should be very careful about following the advice, in text and pictures, set forth in some other books, magazines, and television shows in which the fins are cut off with kitchen scissors. This will work safely on some fish with soft rays, but others have spines that grow into the flesh. These can be dangerous. To remove them (if you must), make a swallow cut with a small, sharp knife blade on either side of the fin. Gently pull the fin out. Then look at it. Any spine on top should have a counterpart sticking down. If it is missing, it's in the flesh and should be removed.

Beheading. To behead a fish, start with a crosswise cut behind the gill flap. Cut through at a slight diagonal down to the backbone. With a stout knife, you can cut on through a small fish's backbone, but with larger ones you may have to make a similar cut on the other side and then break the backbone with pressure applied by hand. In any case, a saw or meat cleaver will not usually be required.

Gutting. It's best to scale and behead the fish before gutting it. To proceed, make a small cut diagonally across the vent. Insert the tip of your knife and cut the skin (from the inside out) toward the big end. Then the guts can be removed easily. The gutted fish can be rinsed inside and out, but arm-and-hammer scrubbing is not necessary. My mother-in-law, God rest her soul, used to scrub all the flavor out of my fish.

Of course, when cutting through the skin it's best not to cut into the innards. This is especially true when the fish belly holds precious roe sacs, which are simply removed by hand.

Filleting. Filleting a fish is not rocket science, but some people do have a problem the first few times. As often as not, a dull knife is a big part of the problem. A fillet knife is not necessary, but they do work better than butcher knives. Most books on fish cookery set forth directions and a drawing or photograph on a common way to fillet a fish, but in reality the savvy angler uses several methods, depending on how he intends to cook the fillet. Here is my take:

> **First Way:** Lay the scaled and gutted fish on its side on a flat surface. Start cutting along the backbone from tail to head, cutting through the rib cage. (Of course, you should cut as closely as possible to the backbone in order to get the maximum amount of meat.) Repeat on the other side. Now you have two rib-in fillets and a backbone. The ribs can be cut out or left in, depending on how the fillets are to be used. Note that these fillets will have the skin on.
>
> **Second Way:** If you want skinless fillets, reverse the process, starting with a cut behind the head and down to the backbone. Turn the knife 90 degrees and cut through the ribs and on to the tail. Do not cut through the skin. Flop the fillet over, using the skin as a hinge, and work your knife along between the skin and the rest of the fillet. This method will yield two skinless fillets with ribs. This is a very popular method used by people who want skinless fillets. Some anglers are adept at this method, often using special electric fillet knives. Note that the fish does not have to be scaled or gutted before the fillet cuts are made. Unfortunately, most people who use this method throw out the head and bones.
>
> **Third Way:** Using a short knife blade, make a cut at the head along the backbone down to the rib cage. Then work your way to the tail. This will yield two boneless fillets, leaving the rib cage attached to the backbone.
>
> **Fourth Way:** This flip-flop technique is my personal contribution to fish preparation. I use the method on eels and long fish such as the chain pickerel and snakehead. To proceed, lay the fish flat on a board. Make a cut in the middle down to the backbone. Turn the knife 90 degrees and cut back to the tail. Flop the fillet half over, insert the knife blade between the skin and the flesh, and work to the end. The forward half is done the same way. This method yields four fillet halves, skinless, and leaves the frame and head intact.
>
> This is by far the easiest way to dress an eel. If it is still alive, it's best to chill it in an ice chest before proceeding. This will keep it from wiggling and make it easier to handle.

Pan-Dressing. "Pan-dressing" is not an exact term, but it means reducing a fish to fit the skillet or pan. With a 2-pound bass or walleye, for example, you may want to fillet one side and cut the fillet in half. Then cut the other side in half. Thus, you will have four pieces. You can, of course, fillet the fish on both sides. Cutting each fillet and the backbone in half will give you 6 pieces. If you have children to feed, or guests who are unpracticed in eating bone-in fish, you can also cut a boneless piece of fish off the end of each fillet, making the crosswise cut immediately behind the rib cage. Also, you can make a cut across the top of the rib section, giving you a boneless finger (a sort of backstrap) of fish from either side. This will give you two boneless tail pieces, two boneless backstraps, two bone-in rib sections, and the backbone. By using this method, you end up with more boneless pieces for the children and guests.

Small fish such as hand-size bluegill are “pan-dressed” simply by scaling, gutting, and beheading them. With the smaller fish, you can merely knock off the scales and fry the rest guts and all, as in A.D.'s No-Mess Shore Lunch in chapter 11.

Appendix II

Cold-Smoking Fish

Fish smoked at a low temperature, usually under 100 degrees, is not cooked. Hot-smoked fish is fully cooked (or should be), which is accomplished at 140 degrees or higher. The gray area in between can lead to problems and should be avoided. Hot-smoking is usually accomplished in large outdoor grills, but cold-smoking requires a special smoker. Several commercial rigs are available, and the jackleg can make his own or improvise. For details, see my book *Cold-Smoking and Salt-Curing Meat, Fish, & Game,* from which this appendix has been adapted.

Be warned that salt, not smoke, is the curative agent in cold-smoked fish. In addition to inhibiting the growth of harmful bacteria, the salt draws out moisture—and moisture is necessary for bacteria to thrive. How much salt and for how long depends on the size of the fish and other factors, and on how long the fish is to be kept before eating. The more salt, the drier the fish and the longer its shelf life. There are two ways to salt the fish, as follows.

The Brine Cure

Although many ingredients are sometimes used in the cure to flavor or preserve the fish, most of these are not necessary and may be counterproductive. I do, however, insist on a little brown sugar in a dry cure and a little sugar cane molasses in a brine cure. The brown sugar or molasses helps the color as well as the flavor of smoked fish. Here's my basic recipe.

1 pound salt
1 gallon good water
1 cup dark molasses

Mix all the ingredients and set aside. Dress the fish and place them in a nonmetallic container, then cover with the brine. Weight the fish with a bowl, stone, block of wood, or some nonmetallic object. This will ensure that the fish remains submerged. Leave the fish in the brine for 12 hours or longer. Remove the fish but do not wash. Let the fish dry until a pellicle forms, a process to be described under a separate heading below.

The Dry Cure

The dry cure should be started by first soaking the dressed fish in a light brine made with 1 cup of salt dissolved in 1 gallon of water for a period of an hour or longer. After soaking, drain the fish but do not fully dry them. Prepare a dry cure by using the 8-to-1 formula below.

8 pounds salt
1 pound dark brown sugar

Mix the salt and sugar. Place part of this cure (about ½ inch) in the bottom of a nonmetallic curing box, then put the rest into a handy container. Place each fish in the salt container, coating both sides. Carefully remove the fish and place it on top of the layer of cure in the box. Layer the fish as necessary, sprinkling extra cure on each additional layer. Leave the fish in the curing box for about 12 hours, or longer for whole fish that weigh more than 1 pound.

Rinse the salt from the fish and dry as instructed next.

Trout smoked to perfection and served with leek and parsley

Forming the Pellicle. Following the salt cure, rinse, pat the fish dry with paper towels, and place on a rack in a cool, breezy place. (Rig a fan if necessary.) Let the fish dry until a pellicle forms, which will be indicated by a glazed film on the surface. This film helps provide a more uniform color, and it may also be an aid in preservation.

Usually, the pellicle will form within 3 hours, but the fish can be dried longer, or overnight, if this is more convenient. Now you are ready to cold-smoke.

Cold-Smoking. The first requirement is to keep the temperature in the smokehouse (or smoke chamber) below 90 degrees, and certainly below 100 degrees. I consider 70 to 80 degrees to be ideal.

You can cold-smoke the fish for a few hours, a few days, or a few weeks. As a general rule, of course, the longer the smoking period, the stronger the flavor. I recommend cold-smoking long enough to form a good mahogany color on the surface, and until the texture is firm but still pliable to the touch.

Properly prepared and duly salted cold-smoked fish can be refrigerated for several days, or frozen for several weeks.

All jackleg chefs will have their favorite woods to generate the smoke, and some will insist on mixing two or even three woods for the proper blend. I like to use pecan wood, partly because I have plenty of it, but I think hickory, oak, apple, or any good hardwood will do.

I depart, however, from the accepted practice of using dry chips or chunks, which are usually purchased at market at high prices. Freshly cut green wood is better, I think, than dried, and it smolders longer.

Index

M

T

About the Author

A.D. Livingston claims to have hopscotched through life. Born and raised on a farm. Navy at 17. Mechanical engineering at Auburn. Atomic bombs at Oak Ridge. Creative writing at University of Alabama. Missiles and rockets at Huntsville. Published a novel about poker and played more or less professionally. Travel editor at *Southern Living.* Freelance writing and outdoor photography. Word Man for bait-casting rods and reels with Lew Childre, the Speed Spool man and genius of modern bait-casting gear. Bought the family farm. Lost the back 40 publishing *Bass Fishing News.* Lost the rest of the farm manufacturing fishing lures. Back to freelancing. Published 20-some-odd books. For the past 16 years—the sweetest of all, he claims—he has been the food columnist for *Gray's Sporting Journal.* What in his previous work experience qualifies him for this position? Nothing whatsoever. He hates to work, but he loves to cook and eat fish and game and he loves to write about it his way.